Ten Years Of YouTube: My Journey

Ten Years Of YouTube: My Journey

Everything I Know About YouTube

Optimus

Published by Tablo

Copyright © Optimus 2022.
Published in 2022 by Tablo Publishing.

All rights reserved.

This book or any portion thereof may not be reproduced or used in any manner whatsoever without the express written permission of the author except for the use of brief quotations in a book review.

Publisher and wholesale enquiries: orders@tablo.io

20 21 22 23 LSC 10 9 8 7 6 5 4 3 2 1

Table of Contents

C1: Introduction	**1**
C2: Building A Foundation	**4**
C3: Creating Content	**14**
C4: Growing Pains (0-1K)	**29**
C5: Establishing Your Roots (1K-10K)	**37**
C6: Scaling Your Audience (10K-100K)	**46**
C7: Establishing Your Brand (100K-500K)	**58**
C8: SEO Basics + Impact	**67**
C9: YouTube Studio	**72**
C10: Collaborating	**78**
C11: Free Resources	**82**
C12: Developing Your Business	**86**
C13: Sponsorships/Brand Deals	**93**
C14: Merchandise	**98**
C15: Titles and Thumbnails	**104**
C16: Copyright & Fair Use	**108**
C17: YouTube Analytics: Reach	**112**
C18: YouTube Analytics: Engagement	**119**
C19: YouTube Analytics: Audience	**128**
C20: What If It Doesn't Work?	**135**
C21: Farewell, and Good Luck	**138**

C1: Introduction

My journey on YouTube has been ten years long, a feat that I never really saw coming. In those ten years, I've learned a plethora of both incredible and useless knowledge that has catapulted me through much of my life to a completely different reality than one I could've ever expected. Instead of a traditional career path, such as working in a factory or spending my life doing office work, I've been blessed with the opportunity to do YouTube professionally.

In this document, I would like to share a comprehensive ten-year-long history, detailing my personal journey throughout this time, the challenges and the setbacks that I've faced, the bittersweet moments and success, as well as the less known side. I'm writing an entire book about YouTube, which means at some points I'll probably get a little bit nerdy. Throughout these moments, I'll be providing you with information that I've used to build a single channel to 1,220,000 subscribers as of me writing this.

We'll talk about analytics, communication with other creators, collaboration, brainstorming ideas, building a brand, growing a full-scale business from YouTube, inside information about the journey, tips, and tricks on how to make your channel more likely to be successful, and much more. In a way, this could be deemed an ultimate 'YouTube book.' Lots of YouTubers write books, and lots of them do it very well. However, *very few* of them are willing to get this deep into the subject.

Before we go further, let me be clear: YouTube is not the easy, money-printing, fame-earning career path for most that you think that it is. Logan and Jake Paul might be superstars, but 99.9% of people can never reasonably expect to even amass 10,000 subscribers. In fact, a study by researchers at the Universities of Amsterdam and Barcelona claimed that out of 36 million YouTube channels studied, only 0.4% of them even amassed the majority of views and subscribers on the platform. 4.4 million channels got past 1,000 subscribers.

This doesn't mean that it's impossible, but it does mean that it is highly improbable. Odds are not in your favor when it comes to doing this professionally - which means you'll need to learn as much as you can and build up as much experience as possible before you even consider growing a YouTube brand.

I'm extremely excited to share all of this information with you all and to have the opportunity to share my story. It means the world to me that people support me enough on a daily basis to not only watch my videos but to go as far as supporting me by purchasing this book. To those of you who've gone out of your way to help push my brand further, I want to sincerely thank you. Without you, this book is not possible, and the story goes much differently.

Without my friends and family, this journey also would not have been possible. To be entirely honest, I hadn't even realized that I was nearly about to hit ten years of Optimus YouTube content until they reminded me that it was coming up. On April 4th, 2012, I started my YouTube journey. I picked the best name possible at the time to represent my brand - ROBLOXandCODvids. It was, of course, a name that I came up with as a child. However, one striking thing about it is that it accurately defined exactly what kind of content this channel was about from the moment you read it.

A lot of your YouTube journey might be noticing subtle things like this, but there is truthfully a science to being a professional YouTuber and performing well on the platform. There is a lot that you must learn to master it and there are a lot of obstacles that will immediately jump out in front of you. If you are not prepared to face obstacles, then you might as well be dead in the water. If you are not prepared to delay gratification, you might as well give up now. YouTube will not become fruitful overnight, and you will not be PewDiePie tomorrow.

This is the first major document I've ever written that I'll be commercially releasing. It is a major venture for me and I'm very excited to have this opportunity to level to you one-on-one about something I've dedicated a lot of my life towards. I love creating content daily and making hundreds of thousands of people's lives even a little bit better. If someone enjoys my videos enough to become inspired, then I feel like I've accomplished a major personal goal of mine. I love to uplift, believe it or not.

Over these last ten years, I've grown a lot. Not only as a person but as a creator. I went from a kid making videos in his bedroom to a man running a business around his dream. Sometimes I wish I could go back to 2017 when I was first blowing up and experience it all again. The journey has given me some of the most surreal feeling of my lifetime. I'll forever remember hitting 1 million views for the first time, reaching 100,000 subscribers, reaching 1 million subscribers, and there are so many other goals I've yet to reach. By releasing this, I'm addressing one of them.

The next chapter of this document will, in detail, explain to you the process of 'figuring it out.' I'll share some insight on how to come up with a channel name, how to figure out what niche you want to target, how to obtain high-quality art or logos, how to research equipment, how to define your content, how to set it all up and how to get perhaps the hardest step of them all out of the way - starting out.

C2: Building A Foundation

I like to think of your beginning stages of YouTube as a foundation. Buildings need a durable foundation that can withstand elements out of their control in order to fulfill their purpose. Like a building, your YouTube channel must have a durable foundation that can adapt to changes in the algorithm, user feedback, new ideas you come up with, and YouTube policy changes. It needs to be a foundation that allows you to consistently provide high-quality videos. It needs to be a foundation that is welcoming to growth and changes in your audience. If you can't build a foundation, how can you expect to grow from there?

First, you'll obviously need to come up with a name. As easy as it sounds, choosing a name for your YouTube channel is actually extremely challenging. Remember, I first went by ROBLOXandCODvids. I've also gone by SmashGaming, Smash, ItsSmash, Adeo Smash, and now Optimus. I did not figure it out the first time, and many people don't. If you later choose to change your name, realize that this comes at the cost of setting you back. If you build a reputation and momentum as someone and then completely switch to a different name, you're going to erase some of your potential gains and take the chance of confusing audiences.

If one day I go by Optimus and the next day I'm DarthVader843, you're never going to know who I am again. This is why it's important to try and nail this the first time. Some people manage to do it, but don't feel discouraged entirely if the name you chose didn't work out as well as you'd hoped. You can change your name and start a different path.

ADEPTOGAMER84024

Long, confusing, doesn't describe anything, extremely off-putting name.

ADEPTO

Short, concise, able to be expanded upon, fits on every screen, clean.

As you can see by this example, the name Adepto is likely to do better than Adeptogamer84024. There are many reasons behind this, but the important ones are listed. Do not choose a long and confusing name unless absolutely necessary. One underlooked thing to notice is that a shorter, more clean name is going to display on virtually all web pages and screens. Long names run the risk of being cut off, so instead of this video being by 'Adepto', it's now by 'Adeptogamer84...', which you do not want. A simple name that can describe you as best as possible is important.

For instance, when I finally settled on 'Optimus', I didn't settle on it due to any personal reason other than I like Latin. In Latin, Optimus translates to 'best.' I wanted to be the best at what I was doing, so I named my channel what I wanted it to be - the best. You should name your channel according to what you want it to stand for most. A channel that has a name that will describe the content perfectly is a great channel and one that can expect to be more successful than a channel with a terrible name.

Once you finally have a few names as your finalists, do a quick YouTube search with them to see what the competition will look like. If you name your channel 'David Johnson', chances are, there are a *lot* of channels out there with that same name. See if any creators with hundreds of thousands or millions of subscribers have already claimed the name. If so, then consider using a different name. You don't want to select a name with a high amount of competitors because when people will search for your content, they perhaps could be led to your new competitors instead.

The name ROBLOXandCODvids was pretty unique but long and unpleasant to look at. The name Optimus has been much more successful for many reasons, and the name of your channel is one of the most important elements.

Next, you want to find your niche. Every channel on YouTube has some form of niche, whether it be a community of creators they fit in with most or even a form of content this channel popularized. For instance, I'm often labeled as a 'commentary channel.' These are channels that provide opinions or takes on a wide variety of subjects. My more specific niche is 'gameplay commentary', where I use gameplay footage as a vehicle to commentate about an oftentimes unrelated subject. This is entirely intentional because I've selected it as my niche. Every single Optimus upload is going to consist of mostly gameplay and commentary. Now, it's time for you to figure out your niche.

If you're looking to make a general form of content, it's best to research the different communities in this type of content to see which category you'd best fall into. If you're reviewing mobile phones and tablets, then it's safe to call you a 'tech review' channel. If you're focusing on makeup and the beauty industry, it's safe to call you a 'makeup' or 'beauty' YouTuber. Finding this niche is one of the most vitally important things you can do for your brand and for your content. It can save you years of time and progress your journey much faster.

I did not always upload gameplay commentary videos. In the beginning, it was primarily gameplay I recorded off the screen of my TV with an iPod Touch in my bedroom. As the years went on, I experimented with a lot of types of content. It wasn't until 2015 that I started doing traditional commentary-style videos on my channel, and even then, it took a further two years until 2017 when I finally had my viral moment that launched everything.

Finding this niche can be tough. Knowing what you want to do with your content, however, should be the main reason that you want to start a YouTube channel in the first place. Don't start it to immediately make money or to become famous, create it so that you can share content with the world. The opportunity to do something like this is a very incredible one, and you shouldn't waste it by not setting your mind to the right part at the right time. Now, you must figure your content out.

For me, I always wanted video games to be a part of it all. I wanted to do gaming content at first, but unfortunately, so does everyone else. Gaming is a very saturated market, meaning that there is a lot of competition. You'll be facing millions of other channels making the same basic type of content as you, all fighting to become viral on a small list of popular games. Most gaming creators want to play what's popular, which leads them all into the same trap. Not diversifying or experimenting with your new content is not a good method for growing.

Testing new things and trying to expand your palette of creating videos is never a bad thing. It could potentially lead you to a breakthrough you've been looking for! Try that new video idea, give the new editing technique a try, or brainstorm new ideas to try and shake up what everyone is already doing on the platform. The truth is, YouTube is a big enough platform for all of us, and it grows every single day. Social media in general is a wonderful tool for you to use to your advantage, and trying new things with it can be exactly what you were looking for.

However, be careful not to just throw any random idea into the mix. Just because things work for others doesn't mean it'll work for you. Attempting to replicate exactly what you've already seen before doesn't leave you with much room to expand and extremely narrows your focus as a creator. Try things that you truly believe will make a difference, not just whatever you think is trendy to do.

So, you've chosen a name and a niche, now you need to consider branding. The most important part of YouTube is learning to catch an eye. Attention spans continue to get shorter, YouTube continues to expand, and all of this leaves you in an awkward position starting out. I no longer have to establish my audience, but in the beginning stages, it gets extremely rough to do. You'll need a logo and a channel banner to truly start a YouTube channel. YouTube gives you auto-generated profile images based on your name, however, these are not going to cut it. People are looking for colorful, vibrant images that accurately represent a brand.

When I first started, I was designing logos and channel banners in Microsoft Paint because I had no money to invest in the channel. I never saw it as a potential cash cow, so I just focused on doing it for fun. As the channel progressively grew, albeit at a slow rate, I quickly realized that having a great logo was going to help grow my channel much more significantly than anything else I could've done.

The Optimus logo has been a blessing for me. For people who've seen it, it has instant recognizability. It's very simple, but it has worked very well over the years that I've had it. The traditional Green Optimus logo on a white background has become the face of my online identity and my brand. My personal advice when it comes to branding is to allow a professional to do it for you. For instance, if you have a good friend who is good at art, consider paying them to design your logo. Also, you can use online services like Fiverr to commission artists to do this for you.

Professional quality branding and logos are going to be a night and day difference between anything you'll conjure up - especially if you're not a graphic designer or skilled in digital art programs. A professional design is going to have marketability automatically baked into it and allow you to grow your brand even more. If your brand isn't somewhat marketable, it is going to be hard to grow. Even if you aren't focused on it as a business, you must realize that certain business principles and mentalities will go a long way. If you want it done right, you'll probably have to pay a little bit for it. Trust me, it'll count where it needs to.

A channel banner is sort of a welcome sign to your channel. This long banner reaches across your entire profile and can be used in a multitude of ways. Personally, I use a basic Optimus channel banner to help solidify my brand more and to confirm that it's the channel you're looking for. Many other good uses of a channel banner are to advertise potential sponsors to your channel, promote other social media accounts to grow them, or show an upload schedule that you're sticking to. Regardless, you need a channel banner. The pros outweigh the cons significantly, and you'll regret not actually taking these steps seriously if you don't.

Next, we'll discuss researching equipment. One of the biggest downsides to starting a YouTube channel is that it can be expensive if done right. To do it right, you'll need to purchase good equipment that allows you to produce high-quality YouTube content in the niche you've defined. This equipment will become part of your brand, which you need to build around your content. There is no bigger element to your content besides yourself than equipment.

For instance, on a daily basis, I need to use the following in order to make an Optimus video: Keyboard, mouse, PC, three monitors, a studio-quality microphone, Adobe software, and audio software to record in. These items alone can cost thousands of dollars, however, you must spend money in order to correctly pursue this. Starting out, you do not need to buy the highest tier equipment possible. As I've previously mentioned, I started out recording gameplay on an iPod Touch and a TV screen. It wasn't 1080p, high definition at sixty frames per second, yet it accomplished the basic task that I needed.

Accomplishing the basics is fundamental to building your foundation, therefore it is extremely important that you do proper research. Watching one YouTube video about the best microphones is not likely to lead you to success. You need to sit down and research your equipment for *hours*. For instance, if you need a camera to record with to make vlogs, here's the baseline on how to research that: Research what types of cameras vloggers often use, research and compare prices, research and compare product reviews, research and compare size and dimensions of the equipment, create a plan for how and where that piece of equipment will be used, determine which few cameras you'll choose between, and figure it out after doing intense research on the product.

You want to make sure that you're getting the best that you can get for your budget. Starting out, you probably don't have an extremely high budget. That's okay because you can make it work. Millions have made it work before and you can do it too. Don't be discouraged thinking that you have to spend $10,000 to even get a start. However, don't be naive and believe that it'll all come with the lowest grade equipment possible. As time goes on and your budget expands for your content, consider upgrades.

Upgrading your equipment can, of course, be costly. However, it is a fundamental necessity for many creators. Equipment breaks and wears out, it becomes outdated and it also sometimes doesn't fit in place with the direction you're taking your channel. This is okay but you'll need to get an idea of how to actually move forward. This can be done by upgrading your equipment. Personally, I tend to replace a good amount of my setup once per year, early in the year. This last year, I replaced my keyboard and mouse setup and got new monitors alongside a new PC. Of course, it was costly, but it was necessary in the long run. To make money, you have to spend money, and making sure that equipment will last and has a purpose is an absolute necessity.

At this point, you need to begin refining exactly what you want your content to be. Don't worry, this is not a ten-second step whatsoever. You'll be refining your content for the entire duration you do YouTube, but at this point, you need to begin the actual process and begin building that future foundation for your channel. Make your first few videos, and don't immediately upload them. This may sound ridiculous, but you want to identify as many problems with your content as soon as possible to not only speed up your journey but to iron out the issues that could set you back down the road. Have some of your friends watch your first few YouTube videos and ask them for feedback. Watch your videos several times over to immediately identify flaws with what you're creating.

For example, what if the resolution of your video isn't consistent with YouTube standards? This can be a big issue. If you notice it beforehand, you can fix it and make your videos much more watchable. What if your microphone isn't picking your voice up clear enough? You now know what to fix in your equipment to make your content better. Finding as many problems as early as possible might sound discouraging, but it's actually a great thing! Now, you know exactly what to target and stomp out of your videos so that they can be much more consumable for a much larger audience.

People do not like videos that aren't high definition, therefore, it's absolutely necessary that you're uploading in 1080p or better. 720p is still somewhat acceptable, but it's going to be extremely challenging to grow a channel while uploading videos less than the standards call for. Sometimes, you can consider uploading in 4K or other options as overkill, but in some niches, this could actually work to your benefit. As part of researching your niche, you should recognize somewhat quickly what the uploading standards are. If you cannot match what your competition is putting out on the most fundamental levels, you're going to be in for a very long and disappointing ride on YouTube.

Which video would you rather watch?

At the same time, try to consider if your content is pushing the messages and purpose that you want. Are you making these videos so you can immediately blow up and profit? Are you making them because you really enjoy this video game? Having this sort of purpose behind your brand and channel is what can make or break a channel. If you're doing something without finding legitimate enjoyment in it, you're going to ruin your perception of doing that thing. If you're making videos you don't like in hopes that you'll get a bunch of attention, you're likely going to make terrible videos that don't entertain audiences.

Image quality and audio quality are crucial to video success. People like videos that they can clearly see and watch that have audio they can clearly hear and understand. Muffled sound, pixelated videos, and more are all problems to look for. If you're making videos and they aren't high quality, you're not setting yourself up for success.

All of these pieces will work together to create the overall foundation of your channel. You need to define what you are and what you make, build a brand around that and use information you learn along the way to refine everything. You need to be on top of as many things as you can with YouTube. You will have to dedicate a lot of time to do this. Nobody ever said that it would be easy.

For my channel, I like to imagine all of these things as big puzzle pieces that fit snugly together. When refining my content, I'm looking for new equipment that will push things to the next level. When defining what my brand is, I'm looking for the best logo and artwork possible. When coming up with a name, I'm using the image of what I want my channel to be to name this. Everything interacts with everything else in very unique ways, and the sooner you map it all out and figure out where everything is, the sooner you'll be on your way to having an established YouTube brand. If you do this right the first time, it'll save you a lot of headaches down the road and boost your initial positivity towards this major project you're working on.

The more that you focus on connecting these elements of your journey together, the better the outcome. You have no reason to delay these processes - not only are they strategically important to complete as soon as possible, but they're the backbone of what you need to have a successful YouTube channel. You'll get nowhere with procrastination. I struggled with this very issue for well over a year, even after establishing my brand. Procrastination and creator burnout are two of the biggest things that you can have to affect your outcome on YouTube. We'll talk about these later in the book.

Next, let's discuss the process of creating content from scratch, how to find video ideas, how to record and edit properly for your videos, how to establish consistency in your content, and how to market content to an audience.

C3: Creating Content

Creating YouTube content is an extremely fulfilling yet challenging process. Most people create YouTube videos for a very limited number of people. For instance, a channel with ten subscribers might just make videos for them and their friends/family to enjoy rather than for six million people per month. In the beginning, it may feel as if you're making videos for just yourself. You'll need to overcome this mentality in order to thrive on YouTube.

Even if you're making videos for nobody currently, you must behave as if you are. You must talk like you have a million subscribers. People need to have a reason to come back to your videos. People need a reason to subscribe and support your brand. If you cannot provide that, rest assured that thousands of other hopeful creators out there will provide that. Viewing your fledgling YouTube channel as what it is can result in you shifting your attitude towards content creation. It's very discouraging to realize you start with 0 subscribers, but every subscriber you gain puts you closer to your goals.

For your first 100 subscribers, you'll probably make bad videos in comparison to what you'll produce as your channel grows. Over time, when a channel continues to gain momentum, you get the chance to gain experience by working on your channel and producing content. By repeating this process repeatedly, even potentially hundreds or thousands of times, you'll gain enough experience to know the process like the back of your hand.

A screenshot of an early Optimus video.

As you can see in that picture, my videos in 2015 (three years into my journey) are not as high quality as they are now. Most of its' views have come from people going back to my older content to see what I uploaded after my channel blew up. This is a great example of repeating a process. I've done these thousands of times now, and as a result, my videos have gotten better. But, in order to get to this place, you must first create and upload *thousands* of videos.

The truth of creating on YouTube is that you must be willing to upload 500 to 1,000 videos before you see results. It can take you forever to begin blowing up on the platform. For instance, I didn't have a viral video for the five years since I was starting. I created hundreds of videos before I eventually saw the success. If you aren't willing to continually create and upload and polish your videos, you're not going to ever get anywhere. Virtually all creators have some level of consistency with their channels if they're running their channels properly. This can mean a few videos per week to start out, but feel free to make more or less depending on what you're looking for personally in your channel.

If you don't create content, you're not going to succeed on YouTube. You have to have the passion and drive to continue to upload and be willing to continue even after failure. It's very unlikely that your first video will hit 1 million views, however, if you continue to upload for 10 views a lot, you'll eventually get the hang of making videos that 100 people can watch. Once you get used to that, you'll notice it gradually increase as you apply other tips and knowledge you gain along the way. Instead of viewing content creation on YouTube as an immediate road to glory, view it more as a long and winding road with lots of bumps and bruises along with it. It's the most realistic way to look at it.

Creating videos won't always be easy, and if you get past the first few steps of creating your channel and begin seriously creating content, you're already on the right path. A creator must provide a constant supply of content in most situations to keep an audience, though specific YouTubers have created upload schedules that can be months long without disturbing their audience. These creators usually have ultra-high production values and create legitimate works of art, though. If you're willing to spend hundreds of hours per video creating the best possible product, then it's entirely possible to get away without uploading often. Otherwise, you need to be uploading content.

At first, I started off uploading sporadically whenever I found the motivation to do so. I'd upload a video after a few days of working on it and immediately move on to the next one. However, this process has changed over the years dramatically. I now produce one video per day on average and try to upload two or three if possible. This is a very stressful, high production uploading schedule, but the brand I've built calls for it. It's become one of the integral reasons that my channel has even become successful in the first place.

Many creators choose to upload a few times per week. Experimentation will help you find an uploading schedule that works for you. You'll need to dedicate a lot of time towards keeping this upload schedule, though. Fans of your content should be able to expect when a new upload is coming in order to pace your structure and to keep them coming back. If you never upload, you're providing new content to enjoy only a few times per year. This is not oftentimes enough to keep an audience captivated enough to want to become true fans of your brand, which they can if you provide enough content for them to consume.

Providing videos that interest your audience is a must. Do not make videos that aren't going to perform well. Stick to what you believe will be the best possible uploads for your channel. For instance, I don't talk about golf tournaments on my channel because I don't believe they'll be good Optimus uploads. I upload videos talking about things that I'm knowledgeable about and things that I'm passionate about. If you cannot find the passion to do this, then you are destined for failure.

One way to figure out what you need to do to make engaging videos is to... watch videos. As lame as this may sound, you'll need to watch hundreds if not thousands of YouTube videos to begin to fully understand what makes a video compelling. When you watch videos, you'll even be able to scout competitor channels as best as possible by watching the content directly and getting a viewer's true experience. Relating yourself to your audience as much as possible is key as these are the people who will keep your channel alive.

Many times, you'll already be watching YouTube content before you even start. In fact, watching my favorite creators at the time is what inspired me to start my YouTube channel back in 2012. If you aren't a fan of the platform or watching content on YouTube, then why are you even starting a channel? You'll need a passion for content creation and YouTube to start your journey. The more content you watch, the better for aspiring content creators.

There are some hurdles in creating content that I'd like to address. One common one is being embarrassed by hearing your own voice. This is something that affected me when I first started

YouTube, as well. Yet, after years of making videos, it has become second nature to me. Like with anything else, consistency is key. Of course, it will sound unnatural and stupid when you first hear your voice on the microphone. It's supposed to. That awkward phase will go away and you'll notice that making videos isn't any harder than you make it have to be.

First, try recording your own voice for about 10 minutes per day in the beginning. Don't show anyone the audio, and don't upload it anywhere. Perhaps use this ten minutes out of your day to record audio notes of plans for your channel. Something constructive would be to keep these audio clips of you detailing your future plans so when you go to put them in action, you have the idea freshly put there for you on something where you cannot forget it. Let's say you want to extend your average video from four to eight minutes long to capture more watch time.

It might be nice for you to record for ten minutes, brainstorming and giving yourself the ideas to put into action later. That way, instead of spending precious time later going through the brainstorming phase, you're immediately ready to move on. Another great way to get used to hearing your own audio is to record yourself talking about your day. A general overview of how the last few hours went not only can be a healthy way for you to vent and let some stress out but also to practice recording yourself and hearing it.

After a few weeks, you'll notice that you won't cringe as much at yourself. You'll naturally adapt to this type of daily routine, and quicker than you think. If you spend the three weeks to get some of the awkwardness out of the way, you can save yourself months of self-doubt and motivation blocking down the road and continue to focus on making your great YouTube content. Why put yourself through more than you need to?

If you record yourself on video, you might also go through an awkward phase where you don't know exactly how to operate the equipment, or you get nervous recording yourself like many others do with just audio. Once again - practice makes perfect. Record yourself talking about anything for 10 minutes a day and this issue will eventually subside, as well. There's no reason to feel awkward if you're about to make good YouTube videos for people to enjoy!

If you have issues working with the new equipment, or learning it, take as much time as possible with the equipment. Another great tool, conveniently, is YouTube. You can find a guide for any piece of technology you can think of on the website, so if some buttons on your camera don't make sense, just search the model up and see. YouTube is also a great source of information in general if you're watching the right content. As you continue to use your equipment and figure out where everything has its' place in your creative process, you'll realize that this is all much easier than the daunting task you thought it would be.

When making content, you're going to initially learn the steps on how to record and make the best content possible, so it's important to learn some tools that you can use to make your content better ASAP. If you're in the need of audio recording software, you can pick up Audacity for free. I've used it for years and stick by it even today. It's a very comprehensive free recording software and it gets the job done at the best price point possible. If you need free software to do thumbnails with, you can consider Canva or Placeit. These places allow you to make decent YouTube thumbnails quickly with a low budget. For editing software, I recommend Adobe Premiere Pro. It has great built-in features and it will accomplish any video editing need you'll have (for most creators.)

Audio is critical to your videos. It's likely that you're able to keep people somewhat interested in a video if the resolution is off or the video is somewhat blurry, but terrible audio will almost guarantee someone to click off your video. Think of an example of a video with terrible audio you've seen. That was annoying to hear, wasn't it? Nobody wants to watch videos where the audio is garbage. Investing in a decent microphone will go a long way for you in the long run.

If filming actual footage, make sure your shot is high quality and satisfactory. Many YouTubers record themselves in their office or computer room, so make sure that you have a good background and decent lighting if filming in an environment like this. These elements of your video are much more noticed than you'd think and can lead to distractions and other negative consequences for your content. If filming outside, make sure the lighting is good and there isn't too much wind or background noise.

If you're interested in creating YouTube Shorts, you must recognize that this is a completely different type of content than what you'll usually post to YouTube. While a YouTube video can be anywhere from 2 minutes to multiple hours, YouTube Shorts are only a minute or less. You have much less time to captivate the audience. You need to immediately stand out. Personally, I did this by creating a separate YouTube Shorts channel last year and uploaded gameplay commentary short-form content there.

These bite-sized versions of videos can be absolutely massive to your overall brand. I would generally consider creators to start strategizing for short-form content as it continues to make a dent in the dominance of long-form video online and is proving to be extremely lucrative to future growth across the board. Feel free to try new types of content with YouTube Shorts, as well! Since a lot of the algorithms and early stages of the program are experimental, you might learn a lot of new information about the platform by doing so.

YouTube Stories is a feature that many creators could use to their advantage and don't. It allows you to create a social media story where you can share updates, news, memes, and links to content straight for your YouTube audience to see. In the past, I've just posted funny memes here, but it can be leveraged really well as a force for hood behind your channel. Use it to promote your newest upload for a few upload cycles and see if you notice any changes in performance.

Another element of YouTube content is live streaming through YouTube Live. The platform is seeing increasingly impressive numbers from live streaming content and live-stream content can generate higher levels of watch time. You also build viewer loyalty as you can directly interact through the stream and make a viewer's day. Many creators report negative impacts on their analytics from excessive streaming, but it has catapulted some creators into a new level of viewership.

YouTube Live works fundamentally a little bit differently than normal videos. It also unlocks different features and monetization options such as Super Chats. Many creators are afraid to stream on their main channels due to the stigma that it can affect the other statistics of their channel. Some people prefer to make separate channels to establish a live streaming side of their brand later down the road. If you're starting YouTube to try your hand at streaming, keep this in mind.

Livestreams and videos also have a much different creative process. While a video lets you refine virtually all details about it, a live stream is just that - live content. You don't usually get to go back and fix mistakes, meaning the importance of quality immediately is much more important. However, YouTube has become well-equipped for aspiring streamers to potentially make a career in the last few years, adding new heavily requested features and implementing more creator tools.

Creating content can be hard, that's why it's important to manage creator burnout. Creator burnout is when a creator overworks themselves, causing them to have a range of responses. Burnout can look like general fatigue and disinterested attitudes or mental breakdowns. There's a wide range that dictates what can happen, but it is a serious issue, nonetheless. You need to find a way to balance creating content for your page with having a healthy amount of time to enjoy your normal life. Getting a regular amount of social interaction is important. Make sure to keep your family and friends close to you so you can always be surrounded by people to keep you grounded.

Some people struggle to manage creator burnout and it negatively impacts their career. Consistently improving your content while managing all the elements of running a YouTube channel is going to be difficult, but there are many ways to approach it to help make it easier. Remember that your mental health matters and that you need to keep yourself in a good headspace in order to be at your very best in all elements of life. After you've learned to manage creator burnout sufficiently, you'll want to continue focusing on making better videos and scaling your audience.

There are a lot of different ways to make sure that you're improving your content. Early on, a tactic I used and definitely recommend is what I call the 'three tries' method. Instead of doing one version of your video, do three separate attempts on the same video and choose from them to select the best version. Make sure to change certain things up in each video to make them different. Experiment with changing the pacing or specific elements of the video to give yourself three videos to choose from.

Eventually, you'll begin to notice patterns by doing this. Many of the things that make the 'best' video you've done will be similar to other content you've made. Maybe you notice that switching the content style up makes for better engagement or by replacing gameplay with a face cam, you've increased watch time. Noticing these types of good patterns in your content allows you to develop a style and routine with your content.

An important element of publishing content on YouTube is realizing when the best time for you to upload is. Typically, this is when the most amount of your viewers are on YouTube at one time, which can vary depending on niche and location. Personally, the best time for Optimus uploads is in the early afternoon. This rides the natural wave of traffic from people getting off work, school, etc. later in the day and gives more time out of the day to generate views.

Making videos can either be a very quick process or an extremely long one. For instance, it only takes me a few hours to complete a video for YouTube, yet some channels spend *thousands* of hours in total to craft the perfect video. Finding out how long on average it will take you to make a video is important for one main reason: it helps you pace your content schedule so that you don't overwork yourself.

If you're spending eight hours a day making YouTube videos, whether or not you make money from it, you're spending as much time as someone would at a full-time job. That is an incredible load of stress to carry on your back. You must prepare for it adequately and figure out how much work you should be putting into videos. Some niches of content will inherently take longer, such as documentaries or short films. Others, like commentary and gaming, might be able to get videos out on the same day.

Something else to consider is the need to learn editing software. In the beginning, you'll likely be editing your own videos by yourself. It's crucial that you take the time to learn editing software to make your videos the best you possibly can. Knowing tricks with this software can make your videos have a production value much higher than they would initially have, which can capture an audience for you. Keeping peoples' attention in your videos is important in every way, so learning to visually capture their attention will be critical.

A major focus you need to realize is that making the content creation process your own is key. You'll need to figure out what inspires you so that you can harness it whenever you can. You need to figure out what elements of creating content you're best and worst at so you know what to improve. You'll find your favorite parts of making videos naturally through the process, and by adding your own little touch to everything you produce, you'll subconsciously build a brand around that.

A big part of my content creation process is creating videos multiple times at once. Since on most days I aim to upload multiple videos, I record everything I need for my videos at one time. For instance, if I need three videos out, I record all the audio for all three videos at the same time to get it all done at once and be able to efficiently move forward in the content creation process. I am also mass-recording gameplay. When playing video games casually with friends, I make sure to record as I'm having fun so that I don't have to intentionally go back and play video games as a 'job.' You can take advantage of this mentality to streamline your process and get more content done faster.

It's had a major impact on my channel personally. I usually can get a day's worth of audio for videos done in about 45 minutes, leaving me plenty of time to go through and edit the videos as I've already usually recorded gameplay prematurely to avoid wasting precious time in the content creation process. By streamlining my process, I'm able to support a multi-upload daily schedule somewhat easier than I'd be able to otherwise. If you begin doing this, make sure to note how much burnout you suffer from and tweak the process to fit you as best as possible.

People love personality. Show the best parts of yourself off in your content. If you're funny, tell jokes. If you're smart, provide opinions. Everybody has their own unique charm that can help them stand out. If you can figure out how to use this to your advantage, it'll be a massive asset. People level with creators they connect with more, as well. If you show that you're a relatable person in your content, then people will naturally gravitate to that.

A great example of a creator like this is PewDiePie, real name Felix Kjellberg. He's one of the most successful YouTube creators of all time, he's the most subscribed individual on the planet and he's fundamentally changed the game with his channel. He's extremely relatable in his content and gives funny reactions to things, so people naturally enjoy his videos. Through this strategy, PewDiePie built one of the largest YouTube empires possible, amassing well over 100 million subscribers and totaling 28 billion views as of me writing this.

Around this time, you need to start considering the negatives you perhaps haven't thought of yet. First off, people are **100%** going to leave negative comments on your content. You will not and can not please everyone. You can, though, learn from the people you do please and use this to your advantage. In content creation, you want to maximize the enjoyability of your video, so you're going to want to read comments and get feedback from your audience. This can be done by reading comments or even by looking through the YouTube Analytics tab.

Analytics will become such an important tool and necessity for you to continue to grow your page. You'll use these insights in every facet of your content creation. To make your audience happy, you need to make sure they are recognized in some way. In the early stages when comments are more scarce, it really helps to read and reply to comments, especially positive feedback or constructive criticism. This not only shows your audience that you care about them and what they think, but it gives you free information to utilize to make your final product so much better.

Also: learn storytelling. If you take the time to learn how to properly tell a story, you'll make your time on YouTube much easier. Someone who can adequately share details in an interesting way will capture an audience's attention much easier. If you work on this element of your videos, you can positively impact your watch time and subscriber counts without even trying just because you naturally captivate an audience more than someone who doesn't have this skill. Editing in a video isn't everything - if you can't give some context and content to an audience in your video, they won't be interested in what you provide.

When you encounter negative comments or spam/bots, you'll have to learn to filter these things out. Our brains seem to navigate these walls of text for the negatives, first and foremost. 100 great comments can mean absolutely nothing if you get one bad comment. This is the sad reality of YouTube - sometimes, you're going to get a nasty comment left on your video. Don't panic or get discouraged, as these are people you likely couldn't convert to fans anyway. It's not the biggest deal in the world.

What you need to focus on initially is becoming proud of your content. Make videos you're proud of. Make content that stands out and highlights you and your creative vision. While personally, my content may not seem like much, I am extremely proud of it. I love making videos every single day. When you get to a point that you love what you produce too, everything immediately becomes more fruitful. Even if a video isn't a million view banger, you're going to feel very fulfilled and happy making it.

Realize that you need to capture an audience's attention and *keep* it. It isn't enough that they clicked the video. They need to watch a significant portion of it for YouTube to continue to recommend your content to new audiences and for you to grow your channel. Many channels have reported a boost in watch time by giving the peak of the video away at the beginning and then working to keep the attention with high-quality, engaging content afterward. Don't let this part of your content get neglected.

Once you've figured out how to capture an audience's attention, you'll start naturally building up watch time on your channel. This is exactly what you want to happen. By learning storytelling, continuing to edit your videos better, and giving great and clear audio, you'll be much more likely to keep an audience interested in your videos. I'm sure you cannot think of one channel that's blown up and stayed successful without learning how to keep an audience captivated.

At this point, you're going to probably want as many people to see your videos as possible. You can start working on sharing your content around and trying to organically grow your reach. If you make content people around you respect, it makes them much more likely to share it with their friends and family, as well. You can grow very well and very organically this way and build a small, grassroots movement behind your channel supported by friends and family.

When you start uploading your first pieces of content that you're proud of, you're now starting the long, winding road we talked about. With your first few videos, you may notice they get tens or hundreds of views, sometimes. This is a good start! While it's slow growth, it's growth nonetheless. Gaining five subscribers per day is better than gaining zero subscribers per day. Around this time, you're ready to start the journey of making content and *promoting it*.

Now, you're focused on getting better every time that you upload and letting your efforts build off one another as time goes on. Many people don't realize how momentum-based YouTube actually is - if you upload consistently, your views and watch time compounding is one of the keys and critical factors to the growth of your channel. Focus on being as consistent as possible (at least once per week is an optimal uploading schedule for most channels to start with.) If you don't realize the compound effect your channel can have, you'll have a harder time understanding your analytics and developing a proper content strategy.

Realize that at the beginning, you likely won't have the best equipment possible to make content with. You're not going to have a camera worth thousands of dollars and a several hundred dollar microphone unless you *know* you can make money from this unless you want to prioritize having the best possible production value off the jump and have an expanded budget. This means you need to learn to 'make it happen' with equipment that likely isn't what you'd prefer. This is okay, most YouTubers have to go through this somewhat awkward phase, but don't forget to prioritize better equipment at some point.

Because you have to start with less-than-ideal equipment, you'll need to be creative. For instance, when I didn't have a capture card to get gameplay, I'd record manually with a camera stacked up on LEGO boxes and books. It was my first way of getting gameplay and is a somewhat common way that gaming channels start off. This wasn't ideal, but it worked, and I scaled my channel to a few hundred subscribers just off this alone.

In the next chapter, we'll talk about how to promote your content best, the best methods of growing fast early, how to share your YouTube channel with friends and family, the early stages of consistency, and how to continue your early momentum forward for a future of prosperity.

C4: Growing Pains (0-1K)

From 0 subscribers to 1,000 subscribers is your first major milestone. All of your initial phases will be taking place in this chapter of your story. Until you hit 1,000 subscribers, you're essentially a nobody. This is okay, though, because the extreme majority of channels never hit this milestone ever. You still blend in with the millions of other channels like you. However, if you build a solid foundation and then create content off of it, you're much better off than the competition. So now, let's use the foundation.

You're going to go through some growing pains at this point. Your channel is still in its' infancy, yet you already feel like you committed so much. Get ready, because the journey is still just beginning. You'll need to continue refining content while also trying to manage growth, which a lot of people can't handle. Now, you're going to start telling people about your channel.

At this point, you're probably safe to start sharing your channel with family and friends. The best part about waiting to do this until now is that it helps you avoid a lot of potential stress. If you make content with the idea in mind that your family will see it, this can subconsciously affect what you make, for better or worse. In this case, you can potentially ruin something great just because you're afraid of what people will say. If you wait until you make content that you personally respect, then it removes all doubt of what anyone else can say.

If people in your personal life don't like your content, then that'll be okay. You like it, and that's what matters most. Also, at this point, you'll have some experience under your belt to potentially combine with constructive feedback that people close to you give you. This can be good because positive words of encouragement from people close to you can incentivize you to keep grinding your content.

At this point in my career, growth was still extremely slow. People in my personal life, especially my friends, all knew about my channel. The issue with this is that I was still making pretty bad videos. This got me made fun of by people constantly. When I was in school, I was often mocked for having my YouTube channel. Because I didn't have a lot of subscribers, people thought that it was funny to make fun of me. Many of the same people have congratulated me now that my YouTube channel actually was successful, which is admittedly a nice feeling. Always believing that you can do it goes a lot further than just being told you can by others. It provides a different type of fuel for you to take advantage of.

I hit 100 subscribers in 2014, which meant I was growing my channel to around fifty subscribers per year at this point. This is not a good growth rate. If you are consistent, you should be able to gain a few hundred subscribers within the first year of you making videos, especially if you can eventually tell friends and family about your channel. Knowing this information now, I want to help you avoid making the same mistakes in this document.

Still, at this point, I never expected this to turn into an actual career. At this point, you'll still be making content entirely for free unless you're able to convert a small audience into Patreon subscribers or you find another way to monetize this content. At this point, you shouldn't be focusing on monetization, but rather on making better content. If you're only a few months in, you're still making objectively worse content than you will be five years in. This is okay, but it's something you'll need to actively consider. Only focus and prioritize monetization when you've figured the rest of the basics out.

There are a few tips and tricks to creating content that we'll go over. These small changes in attitude and workflow can make all the difference. First, let's talk about intros and outros in your videos. Most creators already know what an intro or an outro is, but in case you don't, these are five to twenty-second long segments of your video that help brand your videos and increase the production quality. A YouTube intro needs to be high-quality, descriptive, and to the point in order to catch the audience's eye. Try to keep your intro around five seconds as a good benchmark in order to not discourage a viewer from watching the video. If your intro is too long, annoying, or unclear, it can lead to viewers clicking off your video before you even get a chance to deliver the content to them.

An outro is critical. Personally, I've usually used the outro of my videos to cross-promote. Cross-promotion is one of the most important factors to your overall brand growth. Using these twenty seconds to showcase your other videos, social media platforms, merchandise or other elements of your brand can lead to creating genuine fans of your entire brand and not just your YouTube content. For instance, an Optimus viewer could watch an entire video, enjoy it, and then follow me on Twitter and TikTok because of the outro promoting these accounts. This gives me an opportunity to consistently re-market content to them and to show them all of the other initiatives that I'm working on.

You can find free templates on YouTube and other websites for intros and outros, you can create them yourself very simply or you can pay someone to do it for you professionally. If you don't have any graphic design skills, I heavily suggest paying someone to do it. Not only will the outcome be better but your intro/outro will be much more likely to help convert. You can get a YouTube intro or outro made on Fiverr for as little as $5-10. These types of investments will help you grow your channel significantly.

Next, let's discuss something called workflow automation. On YouTube, you'll have a very unique workflow compared to traditional jobs and careers. As a much more creative job, you'll have more control over everything that you produce than you would on average. Automating the small parts of working on your videos is going to not only take a lot of stress off your back but will significantly speed up the process of creating and uploading content.

One great way to automate your workflow is to use YouTube's built-in features to your advantage. For instance, you can go into your Settings and create an automated description template that YouTube will automatically apply to all of your videos. Instead of spending 15 minutes retyping your description every single time that you upload, consider using this feature to clear up a lot of the tedious work of doing so. Personally, this has saved me 95% of the description writing process as the links to all of my social media are automatically pasted into each new upload's description on my behalf.

~~GOING TO THE WATER PARK AND HANGING OUT WITH ALL OF MY FRIENDS~~

Long, confusing title. Won't display on all devices properly. Doesn't accurately and concisely describe the video.

~~GIONG TO THE WATER PARK AND HAVING A LOT OF FUN WITH MY FRIENDS~~

Long and confusing, has a typo, still not concise enough.

VLOG #01 - THE WATER PARK WAS INCREDIBLE!

Short, to the point, documents a series of content and will display much better.

You can do the same with titles and a few other things that you'll constantly run into. If you're uploading let's play videos, using an automated title might be extremely helpful as titling videos can be extremely tedious and can genuinely be hard work. Getting the right title for your video is crucial. You want to pick a title that accurately describes the video and will display well on all device types. Do not clickbait or blatantly lie in the title of your videos. Not only will audiences realize that you're a liar, but it'll negatively impact the watch time on your channel, which can destroy much of your progress in the algorithm.

Watch time is one of, if not the most important factor for your channel. Watch time is simply the amount of time the combined viewers of your channel spent watching your videos. Average watch time is the key metric you'll be looking for. When it comes to average watch time on YouTube, it's always best to follow the golden rule: the 50% rule. You want your audience, on average, to watch *at least half* of your video. The more watch time you generate with your content, the better.

YouTube recommends content that captivates people. The higher your average watch time, the more YouTube is likely to recommend you. YouTube is in the business of keeping people on its' platform as often and as long as possible. If the average user spends more and more time on their platform, there are more chances for YouTube to advertise to them and generate revenue, not to mention that's less time spent on competitor platforms such as TikTok, Facebook, or Instagram.

Early in my career, the average watch time of my videos was significantly lower. This was for many reasons, including the following: The content was worse, I wasn't uploading videos in HD, I didn't establish a brand soon enough and I wasn't using tips I'd later learn to keep people interested in my videos. For you, this will likely be the same. As you eventually grow to create more watchable content, people will watch for longer, and you'll build more momentum in the algorithm.

As you slowly work to grow your brand and subscriber base, you'll notice that a lot of the things you thought would be impossible with YouTube are slowly becoming more possible. At this point, you'll be working towards YouTube's monetization rules and becoming eligible without even thinking about it. You'll start to slowly build the progress that at one point seemed daunting, and if you can continue to give your project the TLC that it needs, you're going to grow your channel into something very special.

During these growing pains, you may notice that other small creators will reach out for collaboration requests. If this doesn't happen for you immediately, then try moving this outwards and reaching out to other smaller creators to collaborate. Realize that the odds of a channel significantly larger than yours collaborating with you is extremely low, so do not become discouraged if a 100K channel declines a request to collaborate. At this point, find similar channels to yours in size and content type and see if a collaboration is in both of your interests.

Collaborating with other small creators is a great way to build your audience quicker, as well. By collaborating with similar channels with a similar audience to what you want to build, you now have an opportunity to highlight the best parts of your content to a completely new audience. These early collaborations can be critical. Not only do you have an opportunity to expand your colleague list on YouTube and make new friendships but you can significantly grow your channel through this method. Make sure that if you want to collaborate with others that you're giving your best possible effort.

At this time, I was collaborating primarily with my friends who also had YouTube channels. I had a smaller channel compared to some of my friends, so it was critical that I collaborate with them and try to get an audience to grow from this naturally. It worked to a certain extent, and I gained a few dozen subscribers early through this method. While that doesn't seem like a lot, realize that at the beginning you're looking for any growth that you can find. It doesn't have to be a fresh one million subscribers to your channel - as long as the audience remains active with your videos, you're doing something positive.

Another great way to reward your audience during these early times (or realistically at any point in your career) is 'subscriber specials.' These are special videos you create to celebrate hitting a milestone. For instance, I made a Black Ops II minitage video when I hit 250 subscribers, which you'll see below.

> **Celebrate - BO2 Minitage (250 Subscriber Special!)**
> 1,862 views • Jul 15, 2015 👍 69 👎 3
>
> **Optimus** ✓
> 1.22M subscribers
>
> Thank you for 250 subscribers! You're all amazing! I hope you guys stick around for the journey to the future of SmashGaming, to see what we can accomplish. Let's go for 500!

A screenshot of a Black Ops 2 minitage celebrating 250 subscribers.

Good ideas for a subscriber special can be challenging to come up with. A very popular one I've personally employed is a Q&A video. This is a video that allows your audience to ask personal questions about you that you answer so that they can get a better feel for who you are. This also helps because you're actively engaging with your audience and making them feel special by highlighting their questions or giving them an opportunity to talk to you. These usually do very well at accomplishing this task.

This time of your journey is going to be full of great memories later, though it may feel very daunting right now. At this point, I was feeling very negative about my growth on YouTube. Even though I had hit 250 subscribers, I felt like 1,000 was permanently out of reach. If you begin to feel this way, you need to correct it immediately. Success is not immediate for most on YouTube, and your work ethic will scream loudly about where you'll end up. If you allow this to get to you too much, you're going to derail yourself. Keep your head up and focus on growing and having fun.

If you're not having fun with YouTube, you're doing it for the wrong reasons. It's an incredible platform with a tremendous opportunity for you. Don't let your negative thoughts ruin this perception for you. If you grow to hate doing YouTube or you grow to be very negative about yourself and your content, it can permanently destroy everything you've been working for in this time.

You might think that I say this because I've already succeeded, but that's not true. I remember very vividly the multiple years I spent in YouTube purgatory, not growing at a fast rate. I remember feeling down on myself and being made fun of by others for it. It wasn't like I blew my channel up in a few days and never struggled with growth or learning about the platform.

In the next chapter, we'll talk about establishing your brand, the journey past 1,000 subscribers, how to continue the upward trends, what to focus on at this point in the journey, and more. At this point, you're growing semi-consistently, you're reaching new audiences, and you're feeling much better. You've finally broken out a little bit and you're ready to claim your YouTube spot.

C5: Establishing Your Roots (1K-10K)

It's official - you've broken out of the mold and you've gotten past 1,000 subscribers. The awkward stage of your channel is officially over. You've joined the small percentage of channels that reach this milestone, and better yet, you're approaching monetization status. This dream of YouTube being a career path is finally taking shape. You may notice that some of the negative feelings about YouTube are starting to disappear as you've seen more positive outcomes.

This is great! I'm very proud of you, personally. However, the journey isn't over, and you still have a lot of work to do. Just think - to hit 100,000 subscribers, you'll need to do what you've already done 100 more times. This might be too much to think about at the moment, but it's not going to be an easy road ahead.

I got to 1,000 subscribers after uploading two videos in 2016 - my first two successful commentary videos. Amy and Tammy Slaton were in a controversy at the time and I covered it as I would with a typical YouTube video. These videos gained tens of thousands of views and catapulted me from a few hundred subscribers to over the 1,000 subscriber threshold.

A screenshot of the Amy Slaton Exposed video.

At this point, you're going to probably start feeling more confident. If you aren't you should be. You're kicking ass! Now, what's next? How do you move forward from this? How can you keep pushing on?

First, you need to realize what momentum you currently have. If you're gaining subscribers and views rather quickly, you need to focus as hard as ever right now. If you play your cards right, you can blow up and get your momentum to go through the roof. It's time to get serious about this. Don't quit your day job quite yet, but focus a good amount of time on your channel to make sure that you're adequately caring for your project.

Around this time, I started making about three videos per week, at least. When I'd get home from school, I'd head upstairs to my bedroom and work on videos. I'd spend hours making sure the videos came out the way that I wanted them and tried to build up consistency in content creation and defining a workflow. Once I got a pattern down, I was consistently uploading videos that would gain me small amounts of subscribers still. Taking the growth as it came was okay, but it eventually led to me getting discouraged.

This is when I nearly quit YouTube altogether.

In fall 2016, my morale surrounding my channel was entirely deflated. I felt like I was failing like I was wasting my time, and like I'd be better off doing something else. I didn't make videos for months and focused on playing video games with my friends for fun, which was a great hobby to keep myself involved with. At this point, I was jeopardizing my future path with YouTube. I'm so thankful that I eventually changed my mind, but at this point, I never would've foreseen my channel growing ever again.

If you get to this point or have gotten to this point, you'll know that this level of self-doubt can be hard to recover from sometimes. It takes a heavy mental toll on you and your passion for something when you feel like you've failed at it. However, I made a critical and stupid mistake doing this: I didn't give myself enough time to try new things with my channel and to focus on making better quality videos. I was uploading in HD, but I wasn't uploading in 60 frames per second like I am now. This was because I was recording gameplay with the PlayStation 4's built-in recording feature.

When I decided to come back, it took a while. I didn't upload again until the end of 2016 when I was fully committing to commentary. Instead of trying to create some gaming and commentary hybrid channel that focused on two different audiences, I was going to just do gameplay commentary and focus on this niche. My first few videos back did decently well, which was a very huge boost to my morale. It was then that I realized I wanted to do commentary for sure. Ever since then, I've been sticking to the same formula, which has worked for me.

Going into 2017, I fully planned out the future of my channel. I started taking this really seriously as I saw a major opportunity with it. I wanted to make content that I'd enjoy first and foremost, which I was doing well. I now though, wanted to start the race to 10,000 subscribers. I started uploading even more consistently than I was, and in better quality eventually. At this time, I was now growing a little bit faster than before, but still somewhat slow. I wouldn't have gotten to a million subscribers in a million years, but the results were slowly showing.

A screenshot of an early 2017 Optimus upload. I was finally going by Optimus at this time.

To put it as simply as possible, uploading content is the only surefire way to grow your channel. The more that you upload, the more chances you have to strike new audiences. At this point, you'll have an established small audience of at least a few hundred people watching your videos on average. You're finally getting progress towards monetization, and if you've passed 1,000 subscribers, you've now made it past the first milestone:

- Reach 1K subscribers.
- Have 4,000 public watch hours on your channel.

- Have no Community Guidelines violations.
- Have an active, linked Google AdSense account.
- Live in a country where YouTube monetization is available.

If you're able to reach 1,000 subscribers, you're now pushing toward the rest of these goals. Don't upload any content that will violate Community Guidelines, and you'll now have two of the major elements of monetization tackled. Creating a Google AdSense account is free and easy, and will allow you to monetize your videos. You're most of the way there, now. At this point, likely, all you'll need is to get the public watch hours required to monetize your content.

This is easier to do when you're uploading as much as possible. More videos for people to watch means more watch time. More watch time means more momentum in the algorithm. Keep in mind, though, creator burnout is a real thing. While you need to prioritize content, you must find a balance that helps you stay rejuvenated and fresh. Instead of wearing yourself down to the point, you don't even want to upload any more videos, find a great balance that allows you to pursue other hobbies or interests while also getting consistency down.

There's a reason that today, I upload usually one or more videos per day. I try to get 30-40 videos out per month which will allow the maximum amount of watch time that I can currently generate with my content. If I ever get to a point where I can increase or decrease my video production, this can change, but it will not change anytime soon. If you can upload daily, these types of channels get a lot of steam behind them in the algorithm. You can blow up a lot more quickly this way if your work ethic and limits allow you to.

At this point, I started doing subtle things to improve workflow even more. For instance, I created keyboard shortcuts in Adobe Premiere that would allow me to do things much quicker than usual. Instead of right-clicking and finding Delete, I can just press S on my keyboard and delete whatever is selected. It doesn't seem like a lot, but adding little things like this to your workflow can save minutes if not hours on basic tasks. At this point, I've perfected macros and keyboard shortcuts to get things done efficiently and fast.

I also created pre-designed templates to work within my video editing and other ventures. This way, instead of manually editing every last detail of my videos, I have a quick and easy preset for many things that allow me to save time and effort that I'd have to give consistently. Over the years, I'd say this has saved hours of my life in total. If you implement them in the right places, it can save a lot of time for you too.

Side note: In Adobe Premiere, to edit your Keyboard Shortcuts, go to Edit > Keyboard Shortcuts... (Ctrl+Alt+K)

If you're saving even more time by using shortcuts and automating parts of your workflow, you'll deal with a lot less creator burnout and stress. It's a good idea to try and set these types of things up. It'll boost your performance and give you enough room and time to look at other possible imperfections to fix in your workflow and in your content. With this extra time, you can either choose to dedicate more to video uploading or to marketing your content.

At this point in your journey, you're ready for the real work to begin. Now, you're trying to build a genuine platform for yourself. It's time to start trying to grow with other platforms, as well. A great platform to start trying to grow with next is TikTok and YouTube Shorts. Create short, engaging content that will draw people in. Once again, watch time is critical with these platforms, as well. Videos that people can watch multiple times over will be promoted more, so create engaging content that doesn't make people want to swipe away. By doing this, you're now introducing yourself to entirely new audiences, which is great for the stage you're at now.

If you can start building platforms on other social media, you can cross-promote your content to them and turn them into potential fans. If someone is interested in your TikTok content, chances are, they'll enjoy your longer content too. Here is where you're going to notice the difficulties of running multiple platforms at once. It isn't inherently necessary to grow your brand on other platforms, but it can help your growth period be shrunk dramatically if you're naturally good at working on social media and can create a great level of content for people on other websites.

Think of it this way: there are millions of people who are using TikTok but not using YouTube right now. No matter how much your video is promoted on YouTube, these people will not be seeing anything about that. Therefore, it's great to try and convert them by making content on their platform too. Catering to an audience is important. Not to the point where you're selling your whole business away by being a pushover, but to the point where you're inviting potential subscribers and longtime viewers to come and join your community.

At this time, I started cross-promoting my content on Reddit a lot. When I'd make a video talking about a video game, I'd try and post it in its' subreddit to get my video out to an audience that would naturally be more interested in it. This worked tremendously sometimes, and terribly other times. Sometimes, the video just wasn't going to work out anyway. But, when you do strike gold and get a few thousand new views from a subreddit of people who enjoy the video, two things happen. 1.) You just earned new fans and subscribers, and 2.) You just boosted your channel even more with engagement and views you never would've had before.

My blow-up came in August 2017 when I got my first million-view video. A video I had made a few months prior titled *Why I Now Hate Game Theory* was responded to directly by The Game Theorists in a live stream. This gained the video widespread recognition and catapulted it to success. In the immediate months after, I had videos such as *The Day Minecraft Died* and a few

Fortnite videos go viral, as well. This all helped me get from 1K to tens of thousands of subscribers.

By early 2018, I was professionally doing YouTube. I was making good money doing it and my channel was growing faster than ever. Over the years, I've continued my momentum, but it would've all never been possible without my early stages. If I didn't build a solid foundation, I could've never gotten to where I am. It's important to lay the frame down first before you try to rush it all together. By letting things play out, my life forever changed.

Today, I focus a lot on TikTok, YouTube, Twitter, and Instagram. I've grown respective followings on each: 1.2M on YouTube, 92K on Twitter, 22.5K on Instagram, and 44.5K on TikTok. TikTok is especially a big focus because TikTok is exploding in popularity. Each year, more users are joining TikTok that can become potential audience members. Therefore, I've expanded my brand to both short-form and long-form video content to try and grow with two audiences.

TikTok and short-form content are the future of video online. People love digestibility. If something is easy to watch or easy to turn off when they don't want to watch it, it's perfect for them. Instead of finding a new video to watch on YouTube, with a swipe of their thumb, they can refresh to a new video instantly. It's dramatically shortening attention spans. Some people are simply not interested in a 13-minute-long YouTube video. However, they may be interested in a 30-second TikTok. Why lose out on this audience? It's why I focus so heavily on it, and I believe that you should too.

You want to get ahead of everyone else at this point, and many people on YouTube are jumping onto the TikTok bandwagon as we speak. It's poised to be a massive competitor to the major social media platforms for years to come, which has given people the ultimatum: Jump ship and cater to new audiences or risk losing out on the new gold rush of video content online.

When I was in this stage of my journey, we didn't have TikTok. I wasn't really cross-promoting content except for with Twitter, and even then, I didn't really have an audience there. This was a fatal mistake for me that I wish I didn't have to mess up. If I successfully had done this those many years ago, who knows how much different my journey could have ended up?

The truth is - with a healthy TikTok account and a few videos that do well in its' algorithm (which truthfully isn't hard whatsoever), you can easily gain a few hundred or a few thousand subscribers by generating interest on this platform and cross-promoting your content. This, of course, assumes you can successfully pull off a TikTok account. If you cannot or choose not to, then you could miss out on a potential rush of viewership. Also, in my opinion, it adds to the fun of the journey through YouTube to try and branch out and do other things like it.

So, you've done it. You've established your roots, and with hard work, you've gained thousands of subscribers. You're beyond your foundational moments. You're a growing creator with a loyal, small fanbase and you're ready to keep moving forward. It's time to learn about scaling and how to take everything up another level.

C6: Scaling Your Audience (10K-100K)

You've pressed all the way to 10,000 subscribers! You've come so much farther than the average person does with YouTube. Now, it's time to feel proud about what you've created, then, it's back to the drawing board to continue working on the path to success.

Now, you're ready to move on. You've built your foundation, set your roots up, and you're ready to explode now. You may think the journey is over, but you're still far from a creator with a massive following. You have a small town's worth of people following you, though! You've still made incredible strides to get to this point, and I'm proud of you.

Now, it's time to scale. We're going to talk about things that will help you succeed from this point on. If you've been able to get to this point, you have what it takes to get way beyond this point. YouTube is a tricky game, but you're playing it well.

The video that finally propelled me to 10,000 subscribers was my first viral video, *Why I Now Hate Game Theory*. I went from just over 1,000 subscribers to over 10,000 subscribers within a few days. It was completely mind-blowing to me at this point, and my friends were all even more stunned when it happened.

Why I Now Hate Game Theory, my first-ever big video. It has since gained over 3 million views.

For whatever reason, you've built an impressive audience now. You might consistently be getting thousands of views on your videos at this point, which is phenomenal. This is when you really need to take advantage of the momentum you have and go through the roof. Loads of creators hit this point, continued their momentum, and ended up with tens of thousands of subscribers (or even hundreds of thousands) in just a few months.

For some reason, a lot of YouTube channels seem very delicate right at this point. Either you can put the time and work into a channel here and make it turn into something even more phenomenal, or you can give up and let it all go to waste. You've come this far - why not continue and give it your best effort and see what comes of it?

This is when things such as upload schedule and upload quality begin to *really* matter. If you allow your video quality to slack off here, or you begin to upload completely random and unrelated content, you're going to drive away from the audience you spent all this time working to gain. If you don't upload enough, they're going to move onto other channels that actually upload videos and become fans of them instead. If you don't put in the right amount of work at this point, everything can completely unravel.

There have been a few YouTube channels I was really enjoying at this size that completely disappeared from the face of the Earth once they got here. Instead of continuing to push forward, they got complacent and fell off completely. This is still entirely possible. However, there have been many more channels at this point I enjoyed that I've seen explode into popularity after continuing to push forward.

At this point, I knew what opportunity I had personally. And, I wasn't going to let it just run away from me. I had wanted to do this professionally for years, and I knew exactly what I had to do to hit the gas and keep this going. I started uploading as much as I could and got to a point where I was consistently getting 4 or so videos out per week. My audience always had something new to watch, and if they didn't, I was still working on something new. You need to get a consistent upload schedule to keep this momentum going.

Here, you're not even close to out of the growing phase of your YouTube channel. You still have your work cut out for you. If you want 100,000 subscribers, you've gotta do what you just did ten times over. It's a daunting task and it's going to be a lot of hard work. Around this time, you can consider trying to find employees for your channel/brand. If you can find an editor and make more content, consider doing this. Just make sure that it's within your budget that you can afford when it comes to YouTube.

On top of uploading consistently, you should be interacting with your fans on other social media platforms. If you have a Twitter page, consider liking or responding to some Tweets. If you just posted on Instagram, pop in and chat with people under a picture every once in a while. Little things like this can go a long way, not only in building an audience but in retaining one too. People love it when they can interact with their favorite creators like this.

Interacting with your audience makes them want to come back. Not many YouTubers, especially established ones, take the time to respond to comments. At a certain point, responding to many comments will become hard, but you're still at a stage where you can respond to some and see what people have to say. It's a great way to see what audiences think and to increase engagement on your videos, as well. Things like this build YouTube brands more than you think.

When you get to this point, you need to have a consistent content strategy. Random uploads don't usually work, and if they do, it's because that channel is tailored around them. It's best to try and stay active and get as much content as you can out on a consistent basis. This will increase your watch time, give your audiences something to constantly enjoy, and also help you stay heavily involved in your YouTube process.

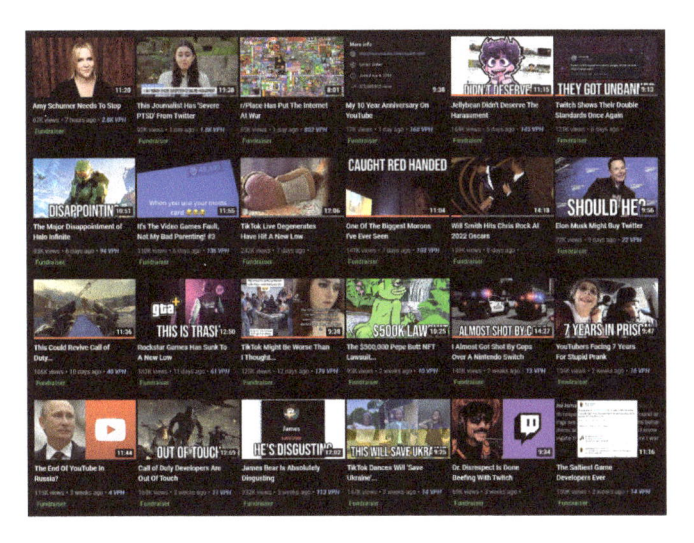

I try to get at least one video out per day or to have one video per day in the month (30 or so videos)

This is when a lot of creators also get stuck in a loop. They try to recapture lightning in a bottle and milk the video or two that has popped off for them. Instead of coming up with new, intriguing, and original content, they focus on making the same video over again trying to pass it off. Don't get to this point. Find new topics to talk about, new games to play, new products to review, or news stories to share. It'll speed your journey up a lot.

People don't want to watch the same video 1,000 times - or do they? Consistency is key, but try to at least have something fresh about every new video you upload. If everything is the same, then things wear out very quickly and people are likely to find other channels that will keep them entertained for much longer. While being consistent, you can find something new to do.

This was when modern Optimus was really starting. I had my content direction picked out, I was finding topics and I was making videos. While many of them never had the success that my initial Game Theory video did, I was able to make some videos I enjoyed and slowly grew my audience again to gain a few thousand more subscribers. This is when, in early 2018, a few videos started doing extremely well that eventually launched me through the rest of this part of my journey.

In early 2018, two videos, in particular, blew up, giving me even more exposure. These videos were *The Day That Minecraft Died* and *Is Fortnite Already Dying?* You'll notice they were both gaming-related uploads, video essays, and around ten minutes long. This is a great formula for content that was popular around the time. Both videos were uploaded on March 5th and April 5th, 2018, respectively. This was a one-month gap in videos that would ultimately hit one million views, catapulting the Optimus channel even further.

The Day That Minecraft Died with nearly 3.7 million views.

Is Fortnite Already Dying? with nearly 1.4 million views.

By mid-2018, I was finally approaching 50,000 subscribers. I was completely stunned by this development. Not only had I never anticipated something like this happening, but it was happening at the perfect time, as well. I was in college and did not enjoy it. I was majoring in computer science and initially had aspirations to work in this field. When my YouTube channel started to take off, this is when that changed and I started to focus more on YouTube. Still, I never took the plunge to drop out... yet.

At this point, I realized that staying focused is what really mattered here. This isn't to guarantee that consistent uploads that resonate with your audience will garner you insane success, but it's definitely a great blueprint to roll with. Remember: you have to have a base, a foundation. A good uploading schedule that keeps people coming back is going to be a great part of that foundation that can lead you to success.

Make sure that at times you still take a chance to consider your videos and your overall brand image. There's always room for improvement. There's no reason to just halt progress because everything is going great now. Don't be afraid to experiment with new content formats and styles to see if you can find anything you like about them. Consider taking a new direction every once in a while and you'll have a lot more fun with your YouTube channel overall.

It's fun to just try new things sometimes. Not only that, but it can lead to new discoveries that boost your content even further! Learning new software techniques is a particular favorite of mine. I like to see how I can twist the shortcuts and other features in the software to make the process as efficient as possible! By doing little things like this, you subconsciously create a level of detail in your creative process that you'll look back on someday and compare to when you first started.

When I first was learning how to edit videos, I was using Windows Movie Maker. Yes, the free software on Windows computers. I wasn't making anything visually exciting whatsoever. Not to disrespect the program, but it just didn't have the functionality that this new software like Vegas or Premiere Pro has. Looking at that compared to today is like night and day. It's a complete difference. Now, it's a legitimate work pattern that earns me the money I need to pay the bills.

If ever, now consider whether or not the staff is in your future plans. The truth is that staff will make it much easier for you to scale. If you can afford some staff, even if one or two extra people work on your projects with you, it'll make a tremendous difference. Not only can you get more content ready and produced but it makes the workflow much more efficient when you can combine great people together on these projects.

Getting a video editor can make a huge difference in your life. It can help your work/life balance so much to just make an investment like this. If you need extra financial support to make a decision like this, then consider starting a Patreon for your fans to support the progress of your channel. At this point, you will likely have at least a few people willing to donate money to help you pay for staff. Even if it doesn't cover all costs, it can be a huge help.

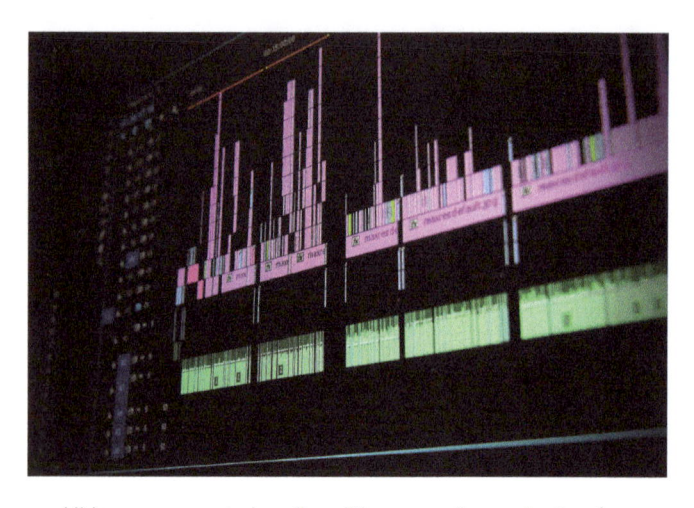

Hiring someone to handle editing or audio production for you can speed up the process while allowing you to make higher-quality content more consistently.

You're wanting to scale here. Getting everything together here can make all the difference. Even if you don't want to hire staff at this point you have to keep pushing forward. More watch time is what you'll focus on. It's important for you to use the Audience tab in YouTube Analytics (Chapter 16) to find out videos that create returning viewers and to see what groups of viewers and audiences you're catering to with your content. By learning your audience here, you're going to have a much easier time down the road scaling. Having the full amount of data you have on your audience thanks to YouTube Analytics unlocks the ability for you to market *extremely* efficiently from here on out.

It will tell you what types of content are working for you. It will tell you what groups are watching your videos, and along with all of the other analytics and data you have, you'll be able to tweak your content strategy accordingly here. By doing so, you can figure out which structured content formats you want to focus on and what types of topics and video types work out best for you. When you repeatedly apply all of this great information, you're going to see good results with consistency and strategy.

Learn how to use YouTube Analytics if you haven't been studying it already. It's going to be a life-saver later in the journey. If you study your analytics often, you can find out so much that you'd never know to help you develop your brand. However, when you start seeing numbers associated with your channel, oftentimes people develop some form of psyche about this.

People obsess over their numbers. If a video isn't the #1 of 10 videos, they'll be depressed. If their video doesn't get 100,000 views in the first 24 hours, they're demotivated. It's a common problem that YouTubers face. It's important to realize that while these numbers are important, you can't value them more than everything. They're important in the sense that you can use them to progress much easier, especially if you take the time to understand them. If you develop a negative emotion with them, you're going to consistently feel burnout and feel demotivated when you're stuck in a dull period of channel growth.

Make sure that you take time away from YouTube. Don't check your analytics every twenty minutes as it's unnecessary. Set healthy boundaries with YouTube so that it doesn't become an overbearing part of your life. This is the reason that many people eventually fall out with YouTube and never end up uploading again. They become too dependent on the good times of YouTube to make them happy. You can't let it affect you personally.

Stressing yourself out at this point can lead to you feeling so unmotivated that you destroy your progress. Make sure to also keep in mind that part of doing YouTube is seeing the ebb and flow of everything. There will be days when your channel significantly underperforms. There will be uploads that don't do as well as you thought they would. These things all happen to creators of all sizes. What really counts is how you bounce back from these things and continue.

Especially at this point in my career, I struggled with this significantly. If a video wasn't the banger I wanted it to be, I felt bad about my channel. I let things like this cloud my judgment on the entire project that I was working on. While this is common, it's important to avoid. I did so by limiting my time looking at analytics to a set amount per day, which also led to me being more efficient when looking through them.

Spending more and more time isn't the key to success on YouTube itself - it's a good level of consistency that helps you tremendously. You want to do the right thing consistently, not the wrong things consistently. If you feel yourself getting overwhelmed, consider a break. Breaks are usually looked down upon in the YouTube scene but it's an important way to keep in touch with your personal life and will help you manage stress tremendously. Currently, I take 3-4 day breaks whenever I feel that I need them and my channel has done fine.

Right now, you're working on scaling your brand to eventually reach 100,000 subscribers. This will be probably one of the longest portions of this entire journey. It's a lot of progress to make, but you've already come this far. If you're able to grow a channel to the first massive milestone of 100,000 subscribers, you've made it farther than almost all YouTube channels.

An underrated and underexploited way of gaining new audience members is to create content for other platforms. Many YouTube channels have exploded in popularity from content uploaded to TikTok. By broadening your horizons and uploading to multiple platforms, you allow access to a whole new demographic of viewers. Plus, many social media users are using more than one platform, allowing you to build a platform that spans multiple platforms. I've done this with YouTube, TikTok, Twitter, and Instagram. It's important to leverage yourself and your videos to make them work across the board.

What I did to start this was I started uploading my content to TikTok. I'd split up ordinary YouTube videos to TikToks, sharing the most interesting segments of my videos to a bite-sized audience. It grew my TikTok platform considerably and allowed me to market my usual content to a new group of users. If you do this properly, you could even gain thousands of subscribers from TikTok and other platforms. Some channels have grown entirely from doing this.

In the next chapter, we'll discuss the path after hitting the 100,000 subscriber milestone, how to establish your brand and identity on YouTube, YouTube Creator Awards, and how things might change a little bit at this point in your career. Nothing ever stays the same forever, and the same principle applies to YouTube.

C7: Establishing Your Brand (100K-500K)

You've made it all the way to 100,000 subscribers! Personally, when I hit this milestone, I actually cried on the live stream for the occasion. It was the biggest accomplishment of my life yet and I was extremely honored by it. This also motivated me like hell to continue pushing forward and seeing where I could take the Optimus brand. Now, it's time for you to do the same.

Channels that make it to this point often will have massive variables that affect how the future patterns of growth will work for their channels. For instance, some creators are officially out of the growth stage of their career and are destined to stay in the hundreds of thousands of subscribers. This isn't a bad thing whatsoever, but some channels are destined to keep pushing the limits to potentially break a million subscribers. Whatever you're happy with is what you're happy with.

My 100,000 live stream on August 16th, 2018.

I hit 100,000 subscribers officially on August 16th, 2018. It was the happiest moment of my life. I had been working on my YouTube channel for six and a half years at this point and never anticipated this ever happening to me. To have this wonderful moment with just over 1,100 of my closest supporters was incredible. You might have experienced something similar when you hit this milestone, as well.

My 100,000 subscribers thank you video.

Let's get back to the topic at hand here. First, let's talk about something which we'll call the 'continued growth' phase. YouTube channels often grow in phases, meaning that they'll have a period in time with extreme growth where they'll skyrocket through the numbers and then have dull periods where growth slows down and things become more consistent. You're focusing on maximizing these extreme growth phases of your channel.

If you want to continue scaling, I cannot stress the importance of hiring staff at this point. If you neglected doing so earlier in your journey, whether it was too expensive or not prioritized, it's important now. You can get away with doing this all solo but your life will be made much easier if you hire people to help with some of the work that running a YouTube channel this size will require. You'll likely need extra hands on deck to continue effectively growing your channel.

This is also a good time to consider having a sponsorships manager involved. They'll negotiate sponsorships on your behalf and add extra revenue to your YouTube channel. Not only can they get you more sponsorships than you're likely to get by doing this solo, but they might also earn you some more money in the process of everything.

At this point, you should clearly know what type of content is working for your channel. How did you get 100,000 people to subscribe without making content that appeals to them? Unless you're one of those '100,000 subscribers with no videos' channels, you're not likely to have zero ideas here. This is great because this means you've already developed a personalized formula that works with your content.

Part of scaling on YouTube is taking that same formula and reapplying it with all of the information you learn through the analytics. Creators who don't pay any attention to these analytics over time run the risk of losing touch with their audience. If you don't know who is watching, you need to figure it out fast. At this point, too, don't be afraid to revisit old videos and see if there are ways to improve them.

In the past, a tactic I've used is to go back and change old video titles and thumbnails to see if any noticeable difference can be made. As time has gone on, I've learned more about YouTube that I can harness than I did then, so I try to update my back-catalog at some times to try and modernize some old videos to see if it can breathe new life into them. Sometimes, this results in noticeable bumps in views and attention on that video.

~~someone stole $100k from people and i'm mad about it~~
Still gameplay frame will not be a good thumbnail. The title was bad.

This Person Stole $100,000 From Everyone
Better, much clearer title and thumbnail.

If you want to focus on retaining the audience you've already built, feel no shame in this decision. You can still make an extremely fruitful career out of a YouTube channel by doing this. In fact, many of my personal favorite channels have taken his route and they make incredible content that continues to bring me back every single time. However, you'll be focusing less on scaling even more and more on consistently remarketing content to your audience.

Know that you'll likely grow regardless. You can still earn a huge amount of subscribers and focus less on blowing up. You won't always need to prioritize getting the most amount of subscribers possible. If it comes with the sacrifice of video quality, then my personal advice is to not do it. Your video quality is one of the most important metrics of your content and can determine whether or not audiences want to come back to your videos. Of course, if you choose to hire staff, this can become less of an issue for you.

Now, I was mostly focused on making content around topics I was enjoying at the time. There was a lot to talk about in all different types of videos. I've always made sure to focus primarily on topics that I genuinely want to talk about. As a commentary channel, this is what I do best. Why talk about things you aren't interested in? I always want to have as much fun as possible while doing YouTube. At this point, doing what is the most fun can also help you make a decent amount of money through your channel, as well.

At this point, you've likely unlocked most, if not all, of the YouTube features. You'll have access to extra monetization features and much more after gaining this many subscribers. You may notice that YouTube will also soon directly reach out to you regarding an invitation to the YouTube Partner manager program. This gives you a direct representative to contact at YouTube in case of any issues.

These managers will also have meetings with you where they help you break down your channel analytics and form strategies for your channel. These have been extremely helpful for me over the years as I've learned all of the new features that YouTube is implementing directly alongside someone from the company. Also, if you ever run into any Community Guidelines or copyright issues, they can help you get through these, as well.

It's always best to try and have connections here. Not only with YouTube and other platforms, but with other creators. Collaborations at this size with other creators can bring in *thousands* of new subscribers from audiences similar to yours. Also, it gives you the opportunity to create unique and awesome videos with your other favorite creators. If you choose not to collaborate, that is also okay as at this size you've already done a lot of your growing and you won't need things like collaborations to get guaranteed channel growth.

Fun fact: My favorite creator to collaborate with is Cyrus.

I was in this part of my journey from August 2018 until early 2020. At that time, I was still rapidly gaining thousands of subscribers, sometimes in a single day. My channel was *exploding*. All I saw was growing numbers, and I was extremely excited. The consistency was paying off! Not only was I getting out consistent uploads, but people were really enjoying them. The average like to dislike ratio on my videos at this point was about 98-99%, which means people were obviously enjoying far more than they were not when it came to my content.

In 2018, I was miserable in college. I was having a lot of fun with the YouTube thing and I didn't see myself in computer science anymore. I didn't enjoy the schoolwork, the schedule, or the general college atmosphere. I figured I was spending money to learn something that I'd never use. So, I made a major decision for my life. I dropped out of college and pursued YouTube full-time.

I knew YouTube is what I wanted to do, but people still judged me for dropping out of school like that. My family seemed extremely disappointed that I made this decision as they'd always expected me to graduate from college. I had done well in school during my childhood (some years, at least) and I'd always had aspirations to continue going to school. However, I had to make this decision for myself and move forward with my life in the way that I wanted to.

Don't take this as an encouragement to drop out of school. I did this because I was in an extremely comfortable situation and I knew that I could make something of it. I had an established YouTube channel that was earning more money than I would at entry level in the career field I was getting ready for. I wasn't just leaving school with no plan. I had a vision of what I wanted to accomplish. Still, the disappointment in me that many held really got to me on a personal level. It upset me a lot.

I continued to work on YouTube, however. As consistent as I could be, I was. I focused as hard as ever because I didn't have a backup plan. If YouTube didn't work out for me, I had to rebuild from the ground up basically. I would have to work a job that I hated or I'd have to go back to school to work in a career field I wouldn't want to work in. I had to focus on this or lose everything I worked for. I was willing to take the risk.

I continued working on my YouTube career for well over a year. I moved out and on my own because of the money that I saved up from YouTube. Had I not had my channel do this well, I could've never moved out this early. This was huge for me because it allowed me to chase YouTube even more living by myself. I didn't have to work around my family's schedule or other circumstances that were out of my control.

I did, however, receive my first YouTube Creator Award, which I earned for getting 100,000 subscribers on my channel. It was a silver plaque, somewhat small, with 'Optimus' on it. It came with a letter from YouTube in a nice official box, and I still have all of my awards to this day. I'm very proud of them and they hang on my wall now.

In late 2019, I began to slack off a little bit. I didn't upload as consistently as I would've liked to, and as a result, I missed a goal I had set up for myself. At the time, I wanted to end the decade with 500,000 subscribers. Due to me slacking and not seeing the end goal and chasing after it, I was about 30,000 subscribers away from the 500K mark when 2020 started. I, of course, took the first opportunity to get back into it and get to work.

This is when my journey changed dramatically. I was still exploding, at least in comparison to my previous growth. I was a little disheartened and beat up about my bad work ethic, and I wanted to force myself to change that so that I could see how this all really could go. That was one of the best decisions that I ever made for my YouTube channel.

I finally hit 500,000 subscribers and started thinking differently. I needed to change up my content strategy a little bit and see what would happen. I needed to experiment with new ideas and see how they would work with the rest of my content. So, I came up with a new content plan and started getting ready to learn everything I could from what I was about to do. I was about to truly commit to YouTube at this point.

In the next chapter, we'll discuss search engine optimization (SEO) in detail and we'll discuss why it's important to your YouTube channel. We'll talk about how it impacts your channel and your videos, how it's important to the growth of your channel and brand, and why you should immediately learn as much as you can about the process.

C8: SEO Basics + Impact

A somewhat underrated and less-discussed element of doing YouTube is how important search engine optimization is. This can impact your channel trajectory in a huge way. Using SEO basics, you'll be able to make your channel much more searchable and algorithm friendly. If you neglect your channel's SEO, you're going to negatively impact your growth.

SEO stands for search engine optimization. It's a critical factor in how websites on the Internet work and how they're discovered in search engines. For example, Google uses these keywords and SEO to rank pages. Pages with more developed search engine optimization are usually ranked higher in the listing, making them more easily accessible and searchable by users on the platform. If you use search engine optimization correctly, the same effect will happen with your YouTube channel and videos.

YouTube is the second-largest search engine in the world. It pulls a ridiculous number of searches per day. Audiences are constantly seeking content on YouTube - new content they haven't seen before. This is good for you and your ambitions as you have a virtually unlimited supply of people to market your content to. Part of marketing that content is learning search engine optimization to further push your videos.

The basics of SEO on YouTube are keywords. These are words that ideally when searched on YouTube or on a search engine like Google, will return results for your content or channel. You can use Channel Keywords to target specific keywords with your channel. Ideally, your name and the names of your most popular content and topics popular on your channel will work fine.

A key to keywords is to cross-reference them. For instance, a heavily targeted keyword I focus on is 'Optimus.' I want people searching for my channel to have the best chance possible to see me and my videos when I upload them. My channel keywords include the name of my channel, the name of many of my most popular videos, topics, and niches that I'm targeting like commentary. By setting these keywords up, my channel has a better chance of directly showing up in search results that are not only relevant but used by a massive audience of people.

When cross-referencing your keywords, include them in the tags of your video. Optimus is the main one that I use. This ensures that whenever someone searches for my channel, not only will my channel page come up, but all of my most recent videos will also show up. Setting up your search engine optimization to display your content for you and consistently recommend you to new audiences is going to go a long way and is one of the main ways to grow on YouTube.

One of the most important elements of publishing a video with great SEO is writing a full, descriptive description. A short description that doesn't detail the video won't work. You'll ideally want one to two paragraphs summarizing the video without killing the interest in the video. Make sure to fill your description full of searchable, relevant keywords and phrases as this can help you in the algorithm, as well. Full descriptions will always be better for your video performance as long as they're relevant.

A great way to handle SEO for your content is through third-party browser plugins and websites such as TubeBuddy or VidIQ. These types of products help you find the best ranking keywords for your uploads, can give you video topics to engage with, and help you unlock advanced looks into your analytics and metadata. They can cost money, though, to get the best potential product possible. This means you should plan to budget for these types of help eventually to help take some stress off your shoulders and improve performance.

Applications and websites like this can be a massive help in getting you accurate information that helps with search engine optimization. Many top YouTube channels use these types of applications, so feel no shame in doing so. In fact, I've used TubeBuddy for about five years now. It's been a tremendous help for me in advancing my career and adjusting my content strategy. These types of plugins oftentimes have free plans, as well.

Good search engine optimization practices will have major ripple effects across your entire channel. Think of it this way: you've been focusing on making your videos more 'watchable.' You've improved your content over time and have much better videos than when you started. Now, you're making your videos more 'searchable.' These two things being majorly improved can be a massive reason why you eventually start to see success with your channel. Continue to work on these things as you grow to continue the snowball effect.

It's important that you're targeting good growth. You don't want to go down the route that some people do where they're buying shady products to try and get an edge or trying to manipulate your numbers. It doesn't work. Focus on bringing in organic, natural growth to your channel. Search engine optimization is key to driving that organic growth to your page. This is especially important if you're making time-sensitive content or videos surrounding trending topics.

A crooked way that many channels attempt to cheat their way to stardom is by buying views and subscribers. Not only is this usually easily detected by YouTube and can make you ineligible for Creator Awards, but it will destroy the reputation of your channel and brand. Trust me, in no circumstances ever do you want to go down this route. You will waste your money every single time. There are many reasons this is the case.

First off, you don't even reap any rewards for this fake traffic. You won't make money, you can't get awards and you won't generate meaningful traffic. Having 100,000 subscribers is great on paper, but when only 609 of them want to watch your content, you're in trouble. Artificial means of growing your platform will do nothing to help you. You will always be better off working on directly building a true brand of loyal followers and supporters.

Second, the risk versus the reward is completely off. We've established that this won't be helpful to you on your YouTube journey, but also, YouTube doesn't take too kindly to people artificially increasing their traffic or 'cheating.' Creating content around this or encouraging artificial channel growth is against the YouTube Community Guidelines, and three violations within 90 days can lead to your YouTube channel being permanently terminated.

Search engine optimization can be intimidating for sure, but you don't need to try and circumvent it. As much of a necessary evil as it can be, it's the best way for you to organically grow your audience, which is exactly what you're looking for. Some things on YouTube are things you'd rather not do sometimes but must do in order to grow. Taking even just twenty minutes per day to research the subject and try to better your skills at it will come a long way.

This is why it's best to just learn search engine optimization. Plus, you can use these skills in other areas of the Internet if you ever choose to expand your brand or potentially even as a job skill in an unrelated field. People who understand how the Internet works and functions at a base level will always be in demand. Many of the skills you'll learn on YouTube are similar - you can use them elsewhere to have a very proficient and successful career in other fields if you just choose to do YouTube for fun and don't pursue making money with it. You can never know too much!

Remember this when you use keywords: focus on relevancy. For instance, if you're making a video about the newest video game out, make sure your tags reflect that. Target the name of the game, the publishers, popular gaming tags, how-to tags, and more to give your video a chance to fully impact the audience you're reaching. The more relevant your video, the better. If you clickbait with your metadata, you're risking your reputation and also turning viewers off the moment they realize you're not telling the truth. Just stay to your topic and focus on healthy keywords that will drive viewers for the long-term, not just tomorrow.

Remember that you want to optimize your channel and videos not just for YouTube, but for search engines. When someone searches 'Optimus YouTube' on Google, I want it to bring my channel up. Many times, it does now. This is what you want to target. If you can be a the top of the search results, you can generate so much more organic traffic. When doing videos about specific topics, you want to outrank all other video content online about that topic. Learning how to use keywords and metadata to your advantage is the most surefire way of doing this.

In the next chapter, we'll go over YouTube Studio and discuss all of its' features. We'll talk about individual tabs, how they affect your channel and how to leverage them to your advantage. We'll take a deep dive into the page that makes a YouTube channel go and figure out how everything fits together to help you progress throughout your YouTube journey.

C9: YouTube Studio

YouTube Studio is where you'll run your YouTube career from. It's the place YouTube has specifically designed to allow creators to view insights and analytics, upload and edit content, handle monetization and copyright, and virtually everything else you'll use for your YouTube channel. It's important to learn the layout of YouTube Studio and to learn what everything does and its' purpose compared to all the other features. The quicker you learn to use YouTube Studio to your advantage, the better.

In YouTube Studio, you'll have a taskbar to the left featuring your Dashboard, Content, Playlists, Analytics tabs, and much more if you're eligible. You can navigate these to access different categories of analytics and features across your content. Each section serves an extremely important function for your channel. Let's do a full breakdown of each.

First, you'll have your Dashboard. This is what will generally load first and is somewhat of the homepage of YouTube Studio. It contains relevant information about your latest video performance, recently published videos, recent Community posts, comments, YouTube Studio updates, analytics, and other important notifications. Many of your most important updates will come to you right here so you can easily access information and make decisions. You can also upload content, go live or create Community posts right from your Dashboard.

Next, you have Content. This will give you a list of all your uploads in chronological order, along with relevant information and monetization statuses. You can make simple edits to content from this page and easily visually compare stats for your videos. You can see information from your videos, live content, Community posts, and YouTube Stories here. You also can change visibility settings with the drop-down menu provided. You can make changes in mass by selecting multiple videos and editing them instead of doing so individually.

Next, you have Playlists. This will show you all of the playlists you've created (or allow you to create playlists) and the number of videos in each. Playlists are a vital part of growing your YouTube audience and can do some of the cross-promoting work for you, so spend time in this tab organizing your content to make it easier for audiences to find. It will also show you when you've last updated a playlist with new content. If you have private playlists for yourself, they'll also show up here.

Analytics is an extremely in-depth and complex set of tools that lets you see the numbers behind your page. In fact, I decided to individually break down the Analytics in chapters later in this book due to the complexity of the tools it offers. Essentially, when researching your channel, this is where you'll be. Your Analytics tab will either be your best friend or worst enemy - if you pay attention and study them, they're insightful. If you become obsessive or don't care enough, they'll be a tool you've lost control of that could be growing your channel and helping you on your journey.

Comments are pretty straightforward. It breaks down comments and direct mentions in posts from other channels, allowing you to see feedback on your content and see what audiences think. You can filter comments here to reply to specific categories of commenters and see their opinions first. It will show you comments across all of your videos by the most recent, so you can use this to your advantage to keep monitoring the feedback across your whole channel. You can also read comments that are published or ones held for review, allowing you to filter out spam and unwanted comments.

Subtitles allow you to directly contribute captions to your own content. It'll tell you how many languages your video has subtitles for, when it was last modified, and more. You can see drafts and published subtitles, allowing you to increase the reach of your videos and make them more accessible to people. Personally, I enjoy subtitles even without hearing issues, so consider this with your content. You can pay people to subtitle YouTube videos if you can find room in your budget to include this. Many creators have had success by working on their subtitles and introducing their content to new audiences.

Copyright is one of the most underrated features in YouTube Studio. It'll show you content matching yours and show you what percent of their video is your content, which can be useful for detecting people stealing your content and taking action. You can also review any removal requests that you've potentially made. If you choose to reach out to creators who've potentially misused your content, it will also document the messages you've sent to them.

Monetization will give you access to all of YouTube's monetization features. It contains tabs with individual options such as ads, merchandise, channel memberships, Super Chats, YouTube Giving, and BrandConnect. You can turn specific options on or off and set up more earning features to increase your revenue. Quickly, we'll break down all of these to give you an idea of what they mean since not all creators will have immediate access to these things.

Ads, merchandise, and YouTube Giving are all self-explanatory. Choose to run ads, sell merchandise directly through YouTube and run fundraisers on your content for charity. Channel Memberships allows you to sell paid monthly subscriptions for extra features on your channel, customizing your price points and perks to your liking. Super Chats are more for live-streamed content and Premieres, but it's when a viewer donates a specific amount of money to have a message highlighted in live chat. This is a useful way to earn money if streaming on YouTube. BrandConnect allows YouTube to directly incorporate brand deals, potentially earning you sponsorship money if a company that can be a good match is found.

Customization lets you edit the public view of your YouTube channel. Consider adding a channel trailer and featured video for returning subscribers in your Video spotlight to give people a view of what your channel and content are like on average. It also contains featured sections, allowing you to promote single playlists or your most recent uploads right on your channel. It also contains a Branding tab, allowing you to add watermarks to your videos and customize your channel banner and profile image. You can also change your channel description, rename your channel and add featured links in the Basic info tab.

The Audio Library allows you to use copyright-free music and sound effects on your videos. This is one of the best features YouTube gives to creators. Instead of risking copyright issues with your content, you can use licensed music via YouTube that will cover you and also allow you to make your content better. You can filter music and sounds by mood, genre, artist, and more. You also can favorite your most-enjoyed sounds so that you can come back to them later.

You'll notice over time that YouTube adds new features to the Creator Studio. It's imperative that you learn these new changes and how to operate these new features as soon as possible. The tools YouTube provides you are truly helpful and delaying usage of these tools is your loss entirely. What you put into YouTube is what you'll get out, and if you put in the extra time to learn these features, it'll help you get a head start on the competition and better your content strategy.

Sometimes, you'll need to use YouTube Studio to make changes to your content. This is when YouTube gets to be the most fun. Here, you have free reign to experiment with your content and the new features that YouTube has given you. The best part is that something you change temporarily can end up having a lasting impact. In the last year, I wanted to drive more traffic across my YouTube channel from people watching. I wanted to turn viewers into repeat viewers.

I started implementing cards and end screens on my videos and statistics have been really positive for repeat viewers, which helped me address a goal pretty easily and effectively. These types of changes may appear subtle and unimportant. If you make these changes often, though, you change the atmosphere around your content and channels in small ways that can have major outcomes for your channel.

By using YouTube Studio's built-in features, I was able to fully strategize, implement and observe the results of this decision. You can do this for virtually anything with your content. Once you break everything down and start to see it as individual pieces that complete a larger puzzle, you can begin to work on things in a completely different way that opens up so many new avenues for you and your channel. However, not everything about YouTube Studio is always sunshine and rainbows.

You might notice that your videos are ranked in YouTube Studio against your last ten uploads. For instance, you might have just uploaded a #3 of 10 video, which is fairly good. However, a lot of creators deal with mixed emotions when they have a poor performance. The key is to remember this number is here to help you, not hurt you. By looking at this, you can figure out what's working and what isn't working for your channel. It might be jarring to see a #10 of 10 videos, but it happens. You have to keep moving forward and upload the next video. If you're a creator struggling with seeing the bad results like this, know that you aren't alone in feeling this way and this system creates a fair amount of problems like this for other creators, as well.

YouTube Studio also has a very useful mobile app. It contains most of the relevant features and information that you'll need (keep in mind that it doesn't currently have everything.) You can use this on the go to see recent video performances or to do some quick research when you have a free minute. I usually use this when I'm away from my computer to keep an eye on my channel and make sure everything is as normal as possible. The app is free to download.

In the next chapter, we'll discuss collaborations and how important they can be. We'll talk about how they can introduce you to new audiences, give you new content ideas, help expand your creator network and give you a new perspective on creating on YouTube.

C10: Collaborating

Collaborations are a great way to add some variety to the otherwise tedious YouTube process. It allows you access to similar audiences, the ability to make great acquaintances and friends through content creation, and the ability to grow your brand doing something you know well. Channels of all sizes collaborate with other channels because it's so important to the YouTube ecosystem. Some channels prefer not to collaborate with others, but those who do end up making great and special pieces of content.

Finding collaborations is about understanding some boundaries: you don't want to collaborate with channels that can't help you grow or give you a great video. Channels that don't make similar formats of content to you shouldn't be often considered for collaboration. For instance, gaming and outdoor fitness isn't necessarily a great mashup for a collaboration unless you can provide a unique challenge or something that will intrigue audiences.

When collaborating, you'll be communicating directly with another creator. This means there can be some disruptions to your usual creative process. Keep in mind whoever you collaborate with will have their own unique style and takes on how things should be done. In order to effectively collaborate, you'll have to be willing to give up some of the control over the video process to make a better product together. The end result will be worth it if you allow the collaboration to truly work.

When asking someone to collaborate, keep a few things in mind:

- Don't collaborate with channels that can't help your brand. You want to have value in the collaboration, and for many, it's the potential growth and exposure of getting a collaboration.

- Don't try and get collaborations with channels out of your league. As rough as it sounds to say - a channel twenty times larger than yours is not going to want to collaborate most of the time.
- Keep it business - don't bother or harass a creator into working with you. Casually approach, keep it business after the agreement is made.
- Meet deadlines. If you're a creator who can't meet a deadline worth jack, you're going to have a hard time collaborating, especially with creators who have their ducks in a row.
- Pitch ideas. Don't leave your collaborator doing all of the work. Think about a project in school: would you want to do all the work for someone else who doesn't care about the project?
- Make sure to promote yourself. If you're a guest on someone's video, don't feel ashamed for adding a small part shouting out your channel or socials. Part of collaborating is trying to grow from it and expand your brand. Creators will understand this.

Collaborating with other channels doesn't have to be any harder than what you make of it. Remember: a collaboration video is supposed to be fun. It's exciting and different to work with someone else, especially if the opportunity really is special and can lead to some positive interactions and growth. Keep in mind that you can always go back and collaborate again with people, as well.

If you create enough good relations with other creators, the word can spread very easily. That way, if creators in your niche and size range are looking for potential collaborators on their channel, you can be a potential target even to new creators. Also, having a list of collaborators can be wonderful for recurring collaborations where you go back and work with people you were already successful with before.

If working on a group project as creators sometimes do, make sure to interact with and communicate properly with everyone in the group. Don't be mean, rude, disrespectful, or a non-contributor. Creators like people that are easy to get along with and easy to work with. If you're not either of these things, you're limiting yourself a lot when it comes to securing collaborations.

Early in my career, I collaborated primarily with my friends. As my channel has grown, I've collaborated with multiple channels. I've jumped into videos for just a few seconds or even outright did entire featured slots for videos. I've had guests on my content, as well. In fact, one of my most popular videos of all time is a collaboration with *dozens* of commentary creators.

Commentary Crusade - Pokimane, the aforementioned video.

If you're on the fence about collaborations, consider the fact that you don't have to have collaborations to have a successful channel. It's simply another element in the mix that can contribute. If you ultimately choose to never collaborate, it doesn't destroy your chances of making it or even making great content. Many creators have never done a collaboration and went on to have extremely successful careers.

In my personal experience, collaborations have been an extremely important and fun part of my career on YouTube. Some of my favorite videos I've ever done were collaboration videos. I enjoy working directly with other people with the same passion as me and I enjoy seeing the final product of what we can come up with together. As often as I can, I collaborate with other creators: if even just a small part in a video.

Next, we'll go over free resources to take your channel to the next level. Whether you're a developed creator or just starting out, free resources can be extremely helpful. We'll figure out how to implement these into our content strategy and build off of them.

C11: Free Resources

Free resources to do YouTube with can be crucial, especially for those of you just starting out. I wanted to dedicate an entire chapter of the book to finding high-quality free resources for creators of all types to use. From thumbnails to editing software to stock images and footage, we're going to break down the best free resources that you can use to up your YouTube game, increase quality and engagement as well as save you money.

Remember that free resources are oftentimes only meant to be consumed during free trial periods or as part of free plans that don't offer you many features. Even though this is the case, you can get a great head start on YouTube and learn a lot just with free software. It can get you to the point where you establish a bit of a foothold, which is where you'll be really better off investing in resources that can do more and bring better results.

Another major issue, especially with free software, is the potential for viruses and trojans on your device. Make sure that you're only using trustworthy software that has a lot of good user reviews. Finding just any software won't work. There is plenty of vouched free software and websites out there to utilize for YouTube content creation that won't destroy your machine to install. Taking the time to find legitimate free software will save you the time and trouble of cleaning your PC down the line.

Many creators fall into this trap. Just because it's free, they trust it. This is why I wanted to compile a list of items that you can use across the board. Many of these I've used myself, but some of them are newer than my time using free software. Please make sure to do your own research, especially if you're using products that I've not recommended in this book. You will thank me and yourself later when things go much better than they can if you blindly download whatever.

The downside of free software is that you get what you pay for. In paid software, you'll have all the features and tools to make consistent high-quality content. In free software, many of these features are oftentimes locked behind premium versions of the software, leaving you with the basics you need to make a YouTube video. You won't get top quality out of any free software, but if you're just starting out, it's something that can help.

First, let's discuss thumbnails. We all know that they're an important part of your video and you need a good thumbnail for a good video, but how can you get great thumbnails cost-effectively? Well, there are a few solutions to this. Websites such as Canva, PicMaker, and Adobe Express allow you to quickly make an eye-catching thumbnail for your video for free. If you can't afford or would rather wait to pay for something like Photoshop, these are quick and effective results for you to utilize.

For free editing software, your options are a lot more limited. If there's anything you should invest money into first, it's editing software. If you're a Mac user, you may have noticed you can use iMovie to make video content. This can be a great starting software. For Windows users, consider free programs such as DaVinci Resolve, Movavi, Hitfilm Express, or Shotcut. You also can go the Adobe Spark route, but if you're going the Adobe road, you might as well go for the premium products as they have more functionality (in my opinion.)

To record audio with your microphone or voice-overs for your content, I personally recommend Audacity. It has all the features you'll need and might be the best piece of free software I use for YouTube even today. Audacity has everything you'll need for this. I haven't even run into paid software that I prefer over Audacity. It's easy to use and works seamlessly with your microphone to produce much better audio for your YouTube videos. It's a must for virtually all creators who will commentate or record audio for their videos.

For stock footage, you can use Pexels or Pixabay. I've used both for various purposes and recommend them highly. The best part about it is the footage and images here are royalty-free, meaning you can commercially use what you find on these websites. For creators looking to grab some stock footage, you can get great, high-quality footage for free and use it for profit. They also host a wide variety of different types of stock footage, so they should be able to meet your needs with just about whatever you're looking for.

For stock images, you can rely on Pexels, Pixabay, or Unsplash. Pexels and Pixabay were mentioned above for their stock video, and the same applies to stock images. Whether you need them to fill up a video or as thumbnails, these websites will be serviceable in finding royalty-free images that you can, once again, profit from without any sort of issues with copyright. This is, once again, something you can budget for. However, when you have resources like this, why not use them?

If you're looking for free intros or outros, you have a lot of options. First, you can find templates uploaded to YouTube very easily and customize these if you have the correct software. Otherwise, you can use websites such as Canva or RenderForest to create effective intros and outros. You can find a decent intro or outro for free - in reality, this is probably one of the easiest resources to find and effectively use for free out of all of these. This will dramatically increase your production value if you do it correctly.

For free YouTube logos and channel banners, you can use Adobe Express, Canva, Picmaker, or Fotor. They offer free templates for you to customize and edit to make your own. When first starting out with no or a lower budget, this can be a great option to help you get an identity and allow you to build your brand early on.

To compare your YouTube channel to competitors and to do competitor research, I heavily recommend Social Blade. It's a free website that will detail everything about a YouTube channel for public consumption. It even gives estimates on revenue and details views and subscribers for you! It has plenty of graphs to show historical data and can be a great tool for researching your channel alongside competitors. It'll also rank you in multiple categories and grade your overall channel performance!

If you're recording gameplay on a PC, you have some decent options to record with. If you have an Nvidia graphics card, I personally recommend downloading GeForce Experience. It allows you to keep your computer drivers up to date and record/stream your screen to your social media pages or save them as clips on your computer. This is how I record gameplay. If you don't have an Nvidia graphics card or want other options, I also recommend OBS Studio for this purpose.

If you need music or audio, you can actually get this for free right from YouTube. If you go into the YouTube Creator Studio and to Audio Library, you'll be greeted with plenty of royalty-free music and sound effects for your video. You can download it directly from YouTube. This is by far the best way for you to find music easily for your content. If you want more advice on this, I covered how to do this in Chapter 9.

Free resources can be huge for you at any period of time throughout your YouTube journey. For instance, I still use Audacity for free today even though I have well over a million subscribers. These types of things are oftentimes seen as 'starter resources', but you can always extend the longevity of these programs if you use them right. It is, however, always better to invest in premium products and software when possible to elevate your YouTube content.

Next, we'll discuss developing the business side of your YouTube page. We'll talk about the steps before extra income sources, do an in-depth dive into different YouTube monetization features, talk about management for your brand, discuss MCNs (multi-channel networks), and much more. Let's unlock the full money-making potential of your channel.

C12: Developing Your Business

You're ready to turn your YouTube career into a money printer. At this point, you're expected to have the following:

- Established channel with at least 50K subscribers.
- Social followings of at least a few thousand on other platforms such as Twitter, Facebook, Instagram, TikTok, etc.
- Money to invest ($1,000 is a good starting number)

You're ready to start growing your business.

YouTube is a really great opportunity to also get into the business world. There's truthfully a lot that you can learn from being a YouTuber that will give you an edge in the business world. If you take the time to research everything, you'll realize that there's a lot more behind your monetization than you think there is.

First, you need to have an established audience. Not a few hundred people, not a few thousand people, but *tens of thousands* of people. If you do not have a large enough following, it's going to hurt you in the business world. The larger your following, the larger brand deals and sponsorships you'll be offered and the more merch you'll be able to sell.

It's important to have the basics down before you start diving head-first into business. First, make sure you've acquired all of the three above. Second, it's time to learn about the potential opportunities for you when it comes to extra income sources. We'll be diving into merchandise and sponsorships in later chapters, but we'll be getting the start down now so we can prepare for these things and effectively release them.

First, let's take a step-by-step look at the many monetization features that YouTube provides channels with.

Advertisements are often the bread and butter of YouTube monetization. Channels that are monetized almost exclusively profit from them. This is likely what you think of when you think of getting your channel monetized. Channels that meet the qualifications for YouTube Premium are eligible to receive better ads with higher-paying rates from Google.

When you first become monetized, you might only have access to advertisements. More YouTube monetization features will open up over time as you pass more subscriber goals. Once you get a channel to about 100K subscribers, you have access to most, if not all YouTube monetization features. If you do not have access to features you think you should try contacting YouTube support.

Channel memberships are another major source of income for some creators. Essentially, members of your audience can choose to pay a fixed amount per month for a membership to your channel, unlocking emojis for live chat and other features that you decide. You can choose between tiers of memberships at different prices with different perks. Some common perks include early access to videos, priority reply to comments, members-only polls in the Community tab, and more.

YouTube channel memberships setup page.

Super Chats and Super Stickers are features more usable for live-streamed content or Premieres. Chat users can pay fixed amounts to highlight their message or to send a pre-approved sticker alongside it to display, giving the user a sense of importance behind their comment and usually allowing the creator to see it much easier. If you're a channel that takes advantage of live streams or Premieres, this can become a handy income source that pays for expenses itself.

BrandConnect is a built-in YouTube feature that allows for brands eligible to work through the service to find YouTube influencers to sponsor. If any relevant deals appear, you'll be able to take them and get paid for sponsorships directly within YouTube. It also offers a YouTube Media Kit, which is a downloadable .pdf file that gives all relevant information to a potential sponsor on one page, expediting the initial process of communication and saving you a lot of time taking screenshots and sending information.

YouTube Giving is a feature that allows you to raise money for charity. You can create charitable events or join public ones, allowing your viewers to donate and raise money for a plethora of causes and valid charities. Through this program, our community has been able to raise tens of thousands of dollars over the years for programs including world hunger, poverty, ocean conservation, Ukrainian support, and domestic violence support networks. You can obviously use this tool to help spread a lot of good intentions and raise money for important causes, including collaborative events with other creators who can join your campaign.

If you're at a point where you're ready to start harvesting these tools to your advantage, then let's start talking about the foundation of building a business around your YouTube channel. You'll want to research potentially trademarking your brand and any original ideas you might come up with as this can save you a massive headache down the road legally. You might also consider opening a bank account with money in it that you only use for YouTube-related expenses and income, making a business account, or streamlining your finances in some capacity.

YouTube will pay you through a Google-owned platform called Google AdSense. Creating an account is free and easy. Your payments will clear if you meet the payout requirements monthly from the 21st to the 24th, on average. This means you'll only be paid once per month from YouTube, so be wise with how you handle your money. If you don't be smart, you can get yourself in a lot of financial and legal trouble.

A good rule of thumb is to save half of it specifically for taxes and unexpected costs, a further 20% for savings and to use the rest how you desire. If this is not possible, tweak the ratios to see what you can realistically afford. Regardless, you will have to pay taxes on your YouTube income at the end of the year, so save for it and don't regret it later. Consider investing a percentage of your YouTube earnings back into your YouTube channel in some way.

Google AdSense oftentimes will send the money as a direct deposit into your bank. If you've partnered with a manager or MCN, you may be paid through them instead. This is if you optionally sign a deal elsewhere while YouTube will directly pay you if you have not.

At this point, it's a fair question as to whether or not you decide to go with some form of management. It can take some of the stress off your shoulders, allowing you to focus directly on your brand and content while the business end of everything is handled above your head. Also, this can help protect you with copyright as any issues you deal with will be argued on your behalf by management or an MCN. They also can pull together sponsorship possibilities for you, as well.

An MCN, or a multi-channel network, is a company that signs YouTubers to exclusive management deals. Often taking 10% or 20% of your total revenue, they'll handle many issues for you. In recent years, MCNs have been increasingly viewed as unnecessary in the creator community. Many of the major examples of MCNs have either gone out of business or fallen on hard times, leading to questions about the business methods of these companies and their trustworthiness after numerous scandals. Many creators will argue that an MCN does nothing significant for your channel while many others still love them.

When it comes to the decision of management, this is entirely up to you. If you want to handle everything yourself, you'll take on more risk, but ultimately it's okay. I personally run virtually all of the Optimus brands by myself, so it's definitely a harder-than-usual job. I have a lot to look over on a daily basis to the point that it's definitely a full-time job.

An important thing to note is that while your audience is on YouTube, you can begin to 'migrate' them to other platforms to have more control over marketing and communication with your audience. Many creators start things such as SMS campaigns or e-mail newsletters to update their audience on new developments, allowing them to directly update their audience on what's going on. We do this with Shoptimus to update our fans on new releases and more.

This gives you much more direct communication with your fans. Instead of relying on YouTube notifications, you can directly notify your audience of what's going on without any issue. Many creators complain that notifications aren't sent out properly and this is a good way to address it. The better connection you have with your fans, the better outcomes will be for your channel. Don't underestimate the power of direct marketing, especially if you grow to include merchandise and other opportunities in your brand plan.

Creating a website for your audience is also a great idea. For instance, I'm building Optiworld, a place for my audience to come and create accounts, share posts, and more. It's like a miniature social media for Optimus fans. This will allow me to directly update my biggest fans on what's going on while giving them a unique experience that most other creators don't provide. This has been done before, with OptTube, as well. Creating experiences like this with your fans that also allow you more direct reach are great ways to help your brand.

The less dependent you are on YouTube alone, the better. Something could always happen that ruins your presence on YouTube, and if you're too dependent on the platform, you can get significantly hurt. This is why I've spread my platform across so many different social media websites. I'm not saying you *have* to create your own website, but it can be beneficial in many different ways to do so.

So, you've got all of the basics down and you're ready to branch out. Remember that you want to research as much as possible before you start committing to anything. First, make sure whatever you have in mind is profitable. If it eats into profit margins or gets too expensive to run, it can jeopardize other elements of your brand.

Now with that out of the way, we're ready to move forward. In the next chapter, we'll discuss sponsorships and brand deals, basic negotiations, discussing price points, bulk deals, long-term brand deals, and earning extra income from being an influencer.

C13: Sponsorships/Brand Deals

You're ready to take on sponsorships. At this point, you can do sponsorships at any point where you have an established foundation. Some companies will sponsor you with a few thousand subscribers while more lucrative sponsorships are given to those with hundreds of thousands or millions of subscribers. Regardless, there's a major opportunity to make money in sponsorships.

We'll go through all of the details, including the negotiation process. This is one of the most business-centered parts of doing YouTube. You will be negotiating prices, potentially thousands of dollars, with people who are complete strangers. These deals can pay your rent or buy you a new car. They can give you the money to invest in your channel and continue growing. They can open up so much financial freedom for you, it's insane. You want to do sponsorships if you can. It's genuinely a **must** for some channels to do this.

Oftentimes, you'll be approached directly by a marketing agency that wants to offer you a sponsorship. These people often take anywhere from 10-20% of the total amount for sourcing the sponsorship for you. This can be an easy way for you to earn multiple sponsorships and see consistent money if you accept. Some of them will want you to sign a deal, sometimes one-year deals, where they're the only ones who can source sponsorships for you. If you want to make consistent money, it's not a terrible idea, but if you want more control over the process, you won't want to do this.

Let's go through an example of negotiating. When negotiating these, deals, you want to always start on the high end. Oftentimes, the person offering the sponsorship is not going to give a direct offer. They want to see what price point you'll give them and what price range they can drive you to. Remember, they're incentivized to pay you as *low as possible*. If you feel like a deal is less than what it's actually worth, consider not taking it unless you can really use the money.

What would you charge for a sixty-second promotion?

I'd like to do $1,000.

That's a little high for us - can you do $600?

How about $800?

We can do $750, but that's it.

Okay, deal. $750.

There's always a chance that you'll get negotiated down in price like this. Don't worry, it happens. You have to be able to make ends meet with companies or provide a really solid offer off the rip in order to get sponsorship deals. Of course, you don't want to oversell yourself and do sponsorships for cheaper than what's reasonable. If you have 500K subscribers, doing a sponsorship for $500 is ridiculous. You could be making thousands of dollars per sponsorship at that point.

You're trying to maximize the amount of revenue that you're generating with your content, not do freebies for companies. **Never** accept an offer where there isn't financial compensation involved. Companies that are reputable and trustworthy will pay you upfront for your services. Sometimes, it is acceptable to take a product as payment. For instance, tech review channels are often sent phones by manufacturers that have a retail value of hundreds of dollars. Not only can you get a new iPhone, but you can get a product review video out fast and cash in off your video, as well.

With my sponsorships, I only promote products that I personally support, and always have. If I wouldn't even consider using it or playing it, I wouldn't sponsor it. You should do the same. I'll never accept cryptocurrency, gambling, etc. types of advertisements on my channel. I'll sponsor mostly anything except for things that I think could negatively reflect on my brand and things I wouldn't consider using or supporting.

When it comes to sponsorships, YouTube is a great opportunity. Remember, when uploading your video, make sure to check the box that says 'Paid promotion' for your video to place a disclaimer on the video of a paid promotion. There's a lot of complex legal jargon about this very topic, and not specifying that you're being paid to promote something can lead to some pretty negative ramifications. It's best to just abide by what you're supposed to do and put a disclaimer here if any sort of sponsorship occurs.

Once you're more established, you might notice that brands want to do deals that extend beyond just one video. Perhaps a company wants to do one sponsorship per month for a year. At this point, you'll be negotiating a **huge payday,** so take this seriously and focus on the opportunity. If you can land three long-term deals, you can financially live free at this point and pay all of your bills just from one income source.

Hello, this is Generic Bottled Water Company. We want to sponsor one video per month for a year. What would it cost to do this?

Normally, I'd charge $1,000 per video. How about we do $10,000 for this deal?

Okay, we'll do $10,000 on this.

A great way to land deals like this is to offer a 'bulk discount.' A bulk discount is a discount that you give for agreeing to do multiple sponsorships over a period of time at once. Instead of getting $12,000 in value out of the individual sponsorships, our example creator will now be getting $10,000. This *is* less money, however, they've now secured $10,000 in sponsorship deals that they'd likely not receive individually. Giving a bulk discount like this encourages a brand to take a risk on your channel and secures you a pretty nice payday, too.

At a certain point in your career, you might be approached by video platforms, streaming platforms, and general competitors about signing exclusivity contracts. These can include Facebook, Twitch, and YouTube. You've likely seen news reports about streamers gaining millions of dollars through these exclusivity deals, which leads me to say this: you likely won't have to worry about this unless you become a major influencer.

However, brands like Facebook Gaming and YouTube Gaming are signing creators on the Internet to lucrative deals, some of which come to smaller creators at smaller rates. If you're ever lucky enough to get an offer like this, it's a major consideration. Are you willing to create exclusive content for these brands? Do you think that it could impact your business? Would the extra money help you grow your brand?

Overall, sponsorships and brand deals can be a major impact on the financial side of a YouTuber's channel. They can be the financial backbone or side cash. They can be something that opens up the possibility of expanding with staff and living solo in a bachelor lifestyle. How you choose to use the money you can make doing this is up to you - but remember that your choices have consequences.

In the next chapter, we'll discuss creating merchandise. We'll go over a general overview, of how to set up an e-commerce store, how to source products, how to find designs, and how to get your products sold to customers you're marketing to through your content.

C14: Merchandise

Okay, you've successfully grown an audience to a respectable size. Before you start implementing this step, I would suggest having no less than 100,000 subscribers. Having merchandise when you have 3,000 subscribers is not only unlikely to be a profitable venture for you, but it may rub an audience the wrong way. You must heavily consider what you do with merchandise and how you choose to approach it.

If you're ready to start merchandise, then you're ready. Now, it's time to learn the basics of what works and what doesn't work with merchandising. Merchandise that you can widely market to audiences include t-shirts, hoodies, hats, coffee mugs, cups, posters, plushies, digital arts, and phone cases. Not only are they very easy to set up but they also are somewhat inexpensive, meaning you can market these much easier. If you were releasing a $500 watch, likely, you won't sell a whole lot. If you're selling a $20 shirt, it's a different story.

YouTube offers channels past certain requirements the opportunity to release merchandise through official partners of the website. These partners include Teespring (now known as Spring), Spreadshop, and Suzuri. There are also dozens of supported merch retailers that you can privately partner with and connect to your channel. This will allow you to create merchandise that displays directly underneath your YouTube videos, allowing the people most likely to buy to directly see it.

An Optimus video with the YouTube Merch Bar feature turned on. You can see multiple products for sale.

If you want to do something more under your control, you can optionally open an e-commerce website and sell your merchandise through that. This can give your merchandise a more branded feel and allow you to branch your brand off of just YouTube. This is where I'll teach you the basics of opening a Shopify store.

Shopify is an e-commerce platform used by countless businesses to create online shops for their products. By doing this and securing your own domain, you'll be able to expand your brand and provide more official merchandising than YouTube's built-in features will allow. You can optionally use a print-on-demand service to warehouse and produce products for you, or you can choose to work out a private deal with a supplier and ship your products yourself.

If you choose to do print-on-demand, you'll have a lot less stress and management to handle. They'll ship your products from a warehouse and your customer will receive your merchandise all on your behalf - however, this will significantly cut into your profit margins as these platforms take a cut of the sale to provide the product and profit from your patronage. Most merchandise from YouTube channels is created through print-on-demand, so don't feel ashamed for going this route.

Shopify has plenty of built-in apps and programs that support print-on-demand, including Printful, Printify, SPOD, Gelato, and Fuel. Each offers its own products and advantages. By using one of these, you'll be able to set up your merchandise much faster. These can be easily integrated with your website by installing them in the store you're running. Once you've done this, you now face the question: what are you going to put on these things?

You'll need to design the artwork yourself or pay someone else to do it. Fiverr is another great place to find artists that can manage this task for you. By creating high-quality artwork that people will want to purchase on merchandise, you've now created your base product. Go into the POD supplier you've chosen and adjust your designs to products and publish them to your store. Price them accordingly, making sure to balance making a profit with affordability. People are unlikely to pay $90 for a t-shirt, so make sure you put decent prices on your store.

Create a comprehensive shipping policy. Shipping will be handled by your suppliers. Make sure to decide between charging customers for shipping or incurring shipping costs to incentivize purchases. In my merchandise store, we incur much of the cost of shipping while customers pay for a minor amount of it. This relieves stress from the customer but cuts into profit margins. This is done because shipping costs have gone up due to inflation and supply chain issues globally after the COVID-19 pandemic.

At this point, consider hiring an artist to create mockups and advertisements for your merchandise. Getting a great mockup can mean the difference between making sales or losing out on potential customers. If you can effectively advertise your merchandise, you're going to have a much easier time selling it. You can also get free high-quality mockup videos and photos at Placeit.net.

Shout your merchandise out in your YouTube videos, on your social media platforms, and in the Community tab of YouTube as often as you can without being annoying. I usually aim for once every 48 hours to not come off overbearing while still keeping a fresh reminder out there that merchandise exists. Of course, running your own merchandise store will require you to come up with your own unique workflow for it.

Merchandise sales are an important cash flow to many YouTube channels. For instance, a purchase at shoptim.us (my merchandise website) supports my channel **10,000x** more than watching a YouTube advertisement. You'll profit much more off of audience members you can convince to buy merchandise. If you consistently release new merchandise, you also can turn customers of the past into repeat customers, increasing their average value even more. Just think - if a huge fan of my channel buys three shirts, that's **30,000x** more financial support to my brand than watching a YouTube ad. It's not even comparable.

Of course, running a merchandise store is only usually fruitful if you've already built a large audience. Obviously, not everyone is going to buy merch, so you have to make sure there's an audience around your channel that is willing to support you like this. Don't be discouraged if you don't sell one thousand t-shirts on the first day - you don't need to cause unnecessary competition for yourself. Be happy that anyone buys it in the first place.

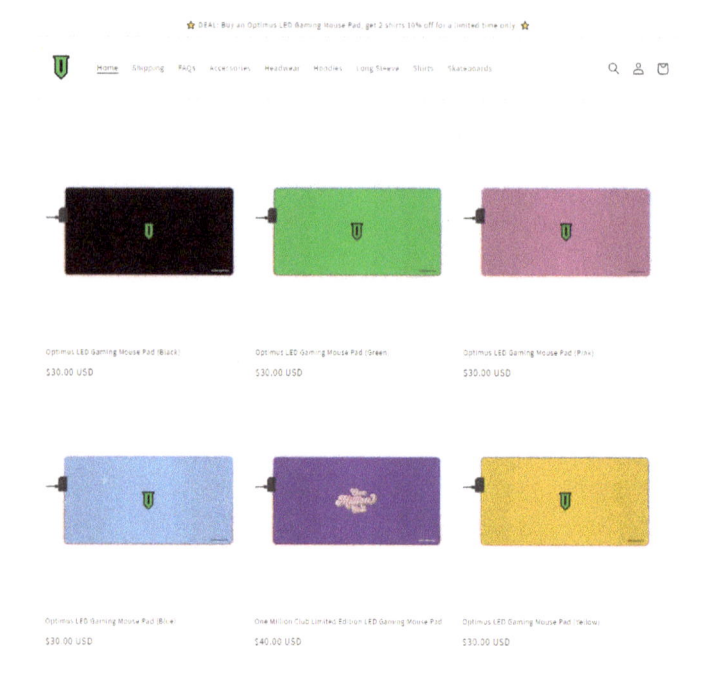

A current image of https://www.shoptim.us (the home of Optimus merchandise)

You want to design your website to convert as much as possible. Consider using one of Shopify's free templates for your website or, if you want to invest, pay for one of the premium templates with more features to look into. I've done both, and I've had great results with both. Also, consider that Shopify isn't the only e-commerce website out there, but it is definitely one of the best and the one that I personally prefer.

In my personal experience, merchandise has been an amazing feature of my brand. My audience supports my merchandise so much, and I'm eternally grateful for that. It's a huge passion of mine to design products that people genuinely are interested in, and with March 2022 officially down, we've broken so many records for our store. The recent release we did (you can see above) was the most popular item we've ever had within 36 hours of releasing them.

Make sure that you're creating products that you're proud of. It's always smart to do sample orders. These allow you to get a discounted piece of your merchandise for you to see the quality and the way that it'll come out for your customers. I've done this multiple times over the years and own a bunch of my merchandise as a result. I get to see firsthand what you'll all be buying, and if I'm not happy, I'm not selling it. That's the same mentality you should have.

Many channels can use this sort of income source. It can financially open you up to upgrading your content, investing in staff, or any other need that can arise for your channel. If you're intent on turning this into a full-fledged business, merchandise will likely be one of the first options that come to you. This is because it's common, it's effective and it's fun.

Merchandising can be incredibly useful for creators of any type. Your content doesn't necessarily matter - if people support your brand, they'll purchase merchandise. If you're a creator who can be often demonetized, market your merchandise as a way to support your channel financially throughout YouTube's demonetization. It'll add an income source for you that can potentially make YouTube your job. Regardless, it's extra money coming into your brand that can be re-invested later down the road to continue expanding.

In the next chapter, we're going to talk about titles and thumbnails. We'll discuss how to create high-quality thumbnails that people want to click, A/B testing, and how to make appealing titles that draw people in.

C15: Titles and Thumbnails

Titles and thumbnails, in a sense, are the gateway to your channel. To a new viewer, these will likely be the first thing that they see of your content. This is why it's important to get these right and optimize them as much as possible. We've already gone over the basics of titles and what to do and what not to do, so let's expand upon the topic and break it down.

Titles have a far-reaching impact on the performance of your video. A weak title is going to turn audiences away from your content. You want to make the most interesting and clickable titles possible. Make sure not to clickbait as much as possible, or at least clickbait in a way that allows you to fulfill what you promise in the title. Never make titles that don't accurately describe your video and its' contents.

Just think - without a good title, you can't have a good video. Think of all the videos you've recently watched. The title was an important factor in you clicking them, right? Because we're not interested in watching videos that won't interest us. An interesting title can literally make or break the performance of a video.

A good way to handle titling is with something called A/B testing. I initially learned about this strategy when I began to upload content to Facebook and have brought it over to my YouTube page, as well. Essentially, create two or three titles for a video that you think are the best possible titles. Then, when uploading, change the title of your video and gauge the performance of the video with each title. Whichever title performs the best, leave it as the permanent title. This gives you options and can change the outcome of an entire video.

T1: Making The Spiciest Ramen On Earth

T2: THE SPICIEST RAMEN IN THE WORLD!

T3: I Made The Spiciest Ramen Possible

You can easily see how each of these titles is different. Experimenting with capitalization, phrasing, and more can make your titles more unique and clickable. Focusing on your titles can be stressful, but it'll make a huge impact on your channel. Instead of only focusing on titling, though, also realize the importance of thumbnails. They work together to provide a clickable experience, so let's talk about how thumbnails intertwine with your title, and let's discuss what makes a thumbnail so important.

Thumbnails are the first impression of your video to most. It's the eye-grabbing image that sums up your entire video at once. Making a good thumbnail has a science to it. First off, you need to make sure you have a high-quality thumbnail. A thumbnail should be at a 16:9 aspect ratio, high-definition resolution (1280x720 or higher), and has a 2MB file size limit. You need to use these guidelines to create the best possible thumbnails. Personally, I prefer my thumbnails at 1920x1080, which equates to 1080p resolution.

You want to create thumbnails with crisp, close-up images. If showing someone's face, make sure that their face is entirely visible and clear to show the facial emotions better and to display better on smartphones and other devices with smaller screen sizes. If you use out-of-focus images or shots that won't look good on smaller screens, you're going to make worse thumbnails than you should be. People naturally focus on faces in thumbnails, as well. If you're the person in your thumbnail, you can also build and solidify your brand by using yourself for thumbnails, which reminds viewers who the channel is and can lead to people coming back more often.

In reality, thumbnails are probably more important than the title in many ways. Since it's a better visual representation of your video, it's something you need to focus on. If adding text to your thumbnail, make sure it's in a readable font and color. Text that is hard to read will turn viewers off of your video and lead to worse click-through rates, which can negatively impact your channel. Make sure to also keep your thumbnails consistent to keep a solid brand image and allow viewers to quickly and easily tell who a video is by.

A tip I use for thumbnails is to display whatever the video is about as best as possible immediately to my audience. For instance, in a video I made about Russia threatening war against Finland and Sweden today, I used the following as the thumbnail:

Here are the reasons that I thought this was a decent thumbnail:

- The text is easy to read and hints to the viewer why Russia made the threats that it did.
- The image of war vehicles shows the severity of the situation and the possible outcome.

- The colors aren't hard to look at and the image is clearly visible.

A major issue with some creators' thumbnails is that they go too far to try and get the audience to click. This leads to them overpromising the intentions of the video with the thumbnail. Click baiting your audience isn't going to be a viable strategy to grow. If your thumbnails are ridiculous and don't accurately describe the content of the video, you're basically giving the viewer a reason to click off early. This can drastically affect your watch time and average view duration, both extremely important aspects of your channel that you want to *maximize,* not *minimize.*

Your titles and thumbnails will work together to create new viewers for you. Not only is it important for growing your audience, but it's also important because it draws back old viewers and keeps people re-watching your videos. Creating a dynamic duo with the two will create videos that are much more likely to go viral. There are countless examples of YouTube channels out there that have perfected titles and thumbnails, one of which being MrBeast.

So, you've learned about titles and thumbnails, A/B testing, the basics of titles and thumbnail performance, what to look for in your thumbnails, and how to create visually appealing, high-quality content for audiences new and old. In the next chapter, we'll discuss copyright and fair use issues. We'll go over the four qualifying factors of fair use and how copyright problems on YouTube work.

C16: Copyright & Fair Use

Throughout your YouTube journey, you will inevitably have a run-in with fair use and copyright. This can be an extremely complex subject for people to understand, which is very understandable. I'm going to try and break this down to not only make it easier to comprehend but also outline the community expectations when it comes to this subject. There are different standards for a lot of people on what qualifies for fair use, so I'll be using the U.S. Copyright Office as a source for the following information.

The Copyright Act of 1976 is currently what dictates much of the copyright law in the United States. It also helps define what fair use is in a legally defensible way. It details what types of uses are allowed under fair use and usually depends on four different factors to help determine if something is fair use:

1.) Purpose of the use - whether commercial or not, the purpose of the usage of copyrighted material can help determine if something is fair use. The goal is to factor this in with the other three determining factors to judge a work regardless of its' status as a commercial work or not.

2.) Nature of the use - How copyrighted material is repurposed is critical for determining fair use. The more transformative a piece of work is, usually, the more likely it will be considered fair use. Generous usage of the copyrighted material is usually seen as more dependent than transformative, which can impact whether or not something is considered fair use.

3.) Amount of work used - Just how much of the original material is used is often the most popular way that YouTubers will justify fair use, but legally, using more of the copyrighted work is generally seen negatively for a fair use argument. If the portion of the copyrighted work is considered crucial to the work itself, this also can hurt a fair use case.

4.) Market for the original content - A defense of fair use generally will claim that the transformative content did not violate the market value of the original work. If a transformative work is deemed to be a sufficient market replacement of the original, it can hurt a fair use case.

Fair use is often evaluated by the individual case. There are little to no official requirements to be fair use and a ruling in court for fair use is often left up to interpretation by the judge. You will likely never have to worry about legal issues with posting a YouTube video, but on the off chance that you do, it's best to seek legal representation with a great history in being knowledgeable about copyright law and fair use. There *have* been cases of YouTube channels going to court over fair use.

On YouTube, fair use is a tricky topic. Many creators refuse to abide by fair use policy and copyright strike videos that are critical of them, use any of their content, or even sometimes mention them in any way. These moves can be malicious, and YouTube doesn't necessarily help by getting involved. YouTube has a basic copyright system - if someone claims your video, you may appeal it. However, the claimant who filed the report is the one who reviews it. Essentially, the people who copyright claimed you get to decide if they were right.

This is so that YouTube isn't held legally involved or liable in any of these cases. As a company, they have to do this. However, it can leave you in a tricky position. It's best to research fair use cases as much as you can if you plan to be a YouTuber, just so that you can be knowledgeable about the situation. Too many copyright issues on your channel can lead to you losing eligibility for some features and even restricted uploading or channel termination.

It's best to be aware of what content you're using on your channel. It's not ideal to use copyrighted video, music, or other elements as it can do more harm than good for your channel. Also, many videos that are copyrighted will have the monetization go to the copyright owner, so you won't be able to profit from the use of copyrighted material. At this point, you're more or less putting your brand and channel at risk and doing damage to yourself.

As a creator, you should be open to other creators repurposing your content as long as it's fair use. Don't be the person who the community grows to hate because you strenuously copyright claim other peoples' videos. If you have a passion for creating content, you should understand that others do, too. Your videos can be better if you allow criticism or repurposing, as well, which could give you feedback on how to improve your content. You can deal with copyright-related issues in the Copyright tab of YouTube Studio.

In the next chapter, we'll discuss the beginning of our deep dive into YouTube Analytics. We'll cover the Reach tab of your Analytics and discuss impressions, views, click-through rates, and unique viewers. It's time to learn about how to grow your channel's reach and attract new viewers to the channel.

C17: YouTube Analytics: Reach

In this chapter, we'll be dissecting the 'Reach' section of the YouTube Analytics page. We'll discuss impressions, click-through rates, views, unique viewers, watch time, traffic source types, external traffic sources, playlist traffic sources, suggested videos, YouTube search, and more.

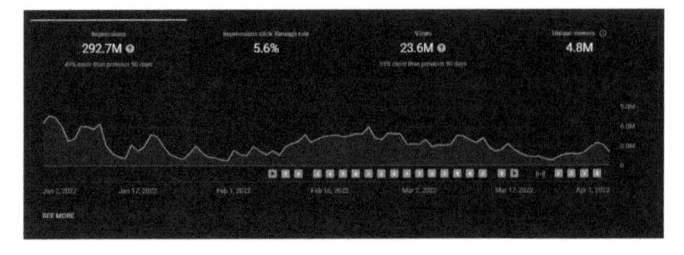

YouTube analytics for the last 90 days. Things are looking pretty good!

According to the screenshot above, the Optimus channel got nearly 300 million impressions in 90 days, which was a 49% increase over the previous 90 days. This is a sizable increase due to more uploads, which have given me an opportunity to have more impressions and more watch time. These things are momentum-based, meaning the more momentum you build, the more momentum you have the potential to build.

These terms might be confusing, especially if you've never seen them before. You might not understand exactly what's going on. That's okay, fear not! We'll be going over what all of this means and help you get an idea of how to use this area of YouTube Analytics.

Let's go over some basic definitions for all of the words in this image:

Impressions: **The number of times that video thumbnails were presented to YouTube viewers only. This does not equate to views.**

Impressions click-through rate: **The percentage of viewers who click on your video when an impression happens.**

Views: **The number of times that videos were watched in a given period of time.**

Unique viewers: **The number of unique people to watch your videos in a given period of time.**

When it comes to impressions, it's something you want to maximize. Essentially, the more impressions you get, the more views you'll get. Giving people more opportunities to discover and click on your content is not a bad thing! This is why uploading frequently and consistently is such a good growth strategy on YouTube. Impressions will continue to grow with more great content!

Your impressions click-through rate is also very important. Essentially, you want to maximize this. The higher percentage of people clicking your videos, the more you'll be recommended by YouTube. This is because the algorithm will detect that your videos are keeping people on the platform and watching content, watching ads, etc. This will incentivize YouTube to promote you even more. My impression click-through rate in this period of time was 5.6%, which was pretty consistent with what I'd expect for my channel. This means out of all impressions, 5.6% are clicked and turned into viewers. You can maximize your click-through rate with interesting, descriptive titles and eye-catching thumbnails.

Your views are what you likely only care about, to a certain extent. Videos with lots of views are highly coveted accomplishments in the YouTube community, especially ones with millions of views. Realize that while views are important, they shouldn't mean *everything*. You want to get high-quality views, meaning viewers who are likely to subscribe and continue to enjoy and promote your content to others. While getting any view counts and is important, realize that the ones who turn into frequent viewers are what you need to have continued success on YouTube.

Unique viewers are one of the coolest analytics available to you. It tells you the unique number of people watching your channel. For me, this is nearly **five million people** in 90 days, which is quite massive in comparison to most channels. By knowing this, you can determine how many videos the average viewer on your channel watches. If you're getting people to re-watch your content multiple times over, chances are, you can turn them into a fan of your channel. Focusing on retargeting the audience watching you but not subscribed is a great way to grow your brand and to build a loyal audience of fans.

TEN YEARS OF YOUTUBE: MY JOURNEY

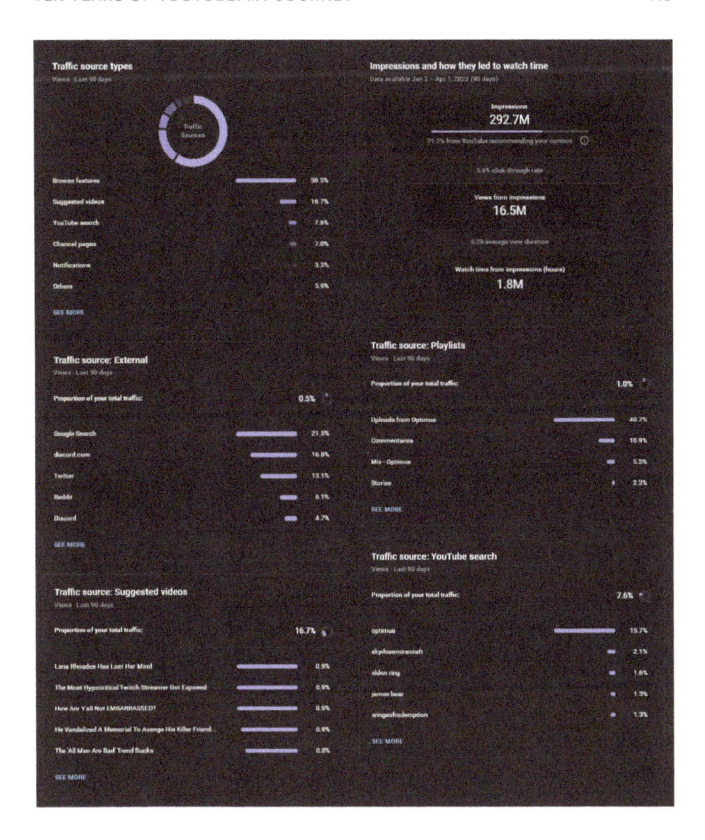

Traffic source types
Views · Last 90 days

- Browse features — 59.5%
- Suggested videos — 16.7%
- YouTube search — 7.8%
- Channel pages — 7.0%
- Notifications — 3.3%
- Others — 5.9%

SEE MORE

Traffic source: External
Views · Last 90 days

Proportion of your total traffic: 0.5%

- Google Search — 21.3%
- discord.com — 16.8%
- Twitter — 13.1%
- Reddit — 6.1%
- Discord — 4.7%

SEE MORE

Traffic source: Suggested videos
Views · Last 90 days

Proportion of your total traffic: 16.7%

- Lana Rhoades Has Lost Her Mind — 0.9%
- The Most Hypocritical Twitch Streamer Got Exposed — 0.9%
- How Are Y'all Not EMBARRASSED? — 0.9%
- He Vandalized A Memorial To Avenge His Killer Friend... — 0.9%
- The 'All Men Are Bad' Trend Sucks — 0.8%

SEE MORE

Impressions and how they led to watch time
Data available Jan 2 – Apr 1, 2022 (90 days)

Impressions
292.7M

71.2% from YouTube recommending your content

5.6% click-through rate

Views from impressions
16.5M

6:29 average view duration

Watch time from impressions (hours)
1.8M

Traffic source: Playlists
Views · Last 90 days

Proportion of your total traffic: 1.0%

- Uploads from Optimus — 40.7%
- Commentaries — 10.9%
- Mic - Optimus — 5.5%
- Stories — 2.3%

SEE MORE

Traffic source: YouTube search
Views · Last 90 days

Proportion of your total traffic: 7.6%

- optimus — 15.7%
- slyphoenixaircraft — 2.1%
- elden ring — 1.6%
- jorson beep — 1.3%
- wingsoredemption — 1.3%

SEE MORE

Don't let this image freak you out. Once again, we'll be going through everything on this page to talk about them and describe why they're important.

Traffic source types: The method YouTube viewers use to find and watch your content.

Impressions and how they led to watch time: This visually filters your impressions down into views from impressions and watch time from impressions so that you can get a better idea of how impressions helped your watch time, an important factor.

Traffic source: External: The websites or programs that are giving you external traffic, usually other social media platforms.

Traffic source: Playlists: The playlists that are leading people to watch your videos the most, usually user-created playlists or auto-generated YouTube playlists.

Traffic source: Suggested videos: The videos being suggested the most from your catalog over a given period of time.

Traffic source: YouTube Search: The search terms and keywords leading to the most impressions and views for your channel.

Traffic source types allow you to know how viewers are finding you. Use this to strategize with titles and thumbnails. Discovery is extremely important for your channel. You want to create content that is able to be easily shared and discovered so you can maximize your channel growth. By studying this, you'll get a better perspective on the growth of your channel and figure out what areas you need to prioritize.

Impressions and how they lead to watch time is incredibly useful. It helps you understand just how impressions are benefitting your channel, and to what degree. You can compare these numbers with the other numbers in your analytics to see what percentage of views and watch time is coming from impressions, which again allows you to strategize growth for your channel.

Traffic sources from external websites are often social media. For me personally, Twitter, Discord, and Reddit are frequent sources of traffic for my channel. This means that viewers are sharing my content most on these platforms and my efforts on these platforms to promote my content are working. You'll often notice Google Search will show up, which is my top source. This is due to people searching topics on Google and being shown your video, therefore watching it.

Traffic sources from playlists detail just which playlists are benefitting you the most. It's apparent that uploading videos in playlists is beneficial, allowing people to bulk watch content or find organized content that they're looking for. Personally, all of my commentaries go into a separate playlist than storytime videos do. This is to keep the channel clean and allow people to see the videos they're truly looking for. Consider employing the same tactic to help your audience find what they're looking for.

Traffic sources from suggested videos help you understand which of your videos are suggested the most by YouTube's algorithm. The idea is to find the elements of these standout videos and replicate them across your uploads. If you notice a certain style of thumbnail performs better than another, consider changing types to try and maximize your views in suggestions. A great title and thumbnail are key in suggested videos because you'll be listed alongside other creators' videos, creating competition.

Traffic source from YouTube search is also extremely important. It shows you what keywords and search terms you should be targeting. If you notice a constant keyword getting you high amounts of traffic, consider putting this keyword in your actual channel keywords in your YouTube settings.

How to go to channel keywords: YouTube Studio > Settings > Channel

Using the Reach tab of your YouTube Analytics page will help you understand more about your audience, your potential audience, what sources of traffic you're getting, and what you should be targeting as a creator. It is very important to constantly check analytics like this to see the consistent changes or to note any new trends. If you use this tab correctly and learn how to navigate it perfectly, you're going to have a great recipe for success in targeting new audiences on YouTube and spreading your reach even further.

In the next chapter, we'll discuss the Engagement tab of YouTube Analytics and discuss watch time, average view duration, key moments for audience retention, top videos, and more. We'll go over why engagement is important, how to maximize your engagement and how to push your channel's performance even further to reap more rewards for you.

C18: YouTube Analytics: Engagement

Engagement is critical to the success of a YouTube channel. Put simply, engagement is anytime that a viewer interacts with your video (like/dislike, sharing, comments, etc.) You'll need significant amounts of engagement to continue being recommended by YouTube. If the audience interacts with your videos more than the average video, YouTube sees that as a sign that your video is highly enjoyable and marketable.

In this chapter, we're going to break it all down and dissect it so that we can figure out how to maximize our engagement and how to read the information provided by YouTube to strategize and adapt. Doing so will give you an inherent advantage over your competition and allow you to fully plan the direction you want to take your channel in. Failing to maximize engagement will set you back.

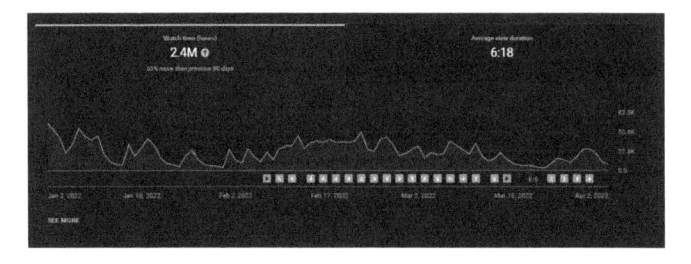

The main view of your Engagement tab. You'll notice watch time in hours and average view duration.

Let's go over the terms for our Engagement tab:

Watch time (hours): The number of hours spent watching your content in a given period of time.

Average view duration: The average time spent watching your videos by the average user.

Key moments for audience retention: The percent of viewers still watching your video at the 30-second mark. This allows you to see which videos are keeping peoples' attention the most and strategize from them.

Top videos: Your best performing videos based on watch time in a given period of time.

Top posts: Your best performing Community posts in a given period of time. You can base this on Image posts, Poll posts, Text posts, and Video posts.

Top playlists: The playlists generating the most watch time for your channel in a given period of time.

Top videos by end screen: The videos with the most effective end screens. It will show how many clicks they've generated per video. This is important for cross-promoting content specifically on YouTube.

Top cards: The best performing cards in a given period of time.

Top end screen element types: The type of end screens that perform the best on your videos.

A screenshot of much of the Engagement tab in YouTube Analytics.

Reading these analytics is crucial. You want to have as much engagement as possible. Even negative engagement such as dislikes is important. If someone dislikes your video, what can you immediately pull from such negative feedback? What can you learn from a nasty comment being left on your video?

- Perhaps your video quality is too low.
- Maybe you've said something too controversial.
- You could just have had an unlucky encounter with this viewer.

Taking negative feedback through engagement not only helps you solidify your content more, but also helps you in recommendations. YouTube is looking to promote content that gets people to interact, as it shows this video is able to keep someone's attention. It doesn't matter if it's good or bad. If someone dislikes your video, it's still going to work in your favor. While you shouldn't seek out negative interactions with the audience, you can still benefit from them tremendously.

Watch time is the true backbone of your channel. Many think that views and subscribers are the only numbers that really count - this is far from the truth. Your watch time is the primary factor that YouTube is going to use in promoting your content. You want to maximize watch time. Perhaps encourage the viewer to watch the entire video early on in the video so that they're audibly or visually incentivized and reminded to watch more of the video. By doing so, you can increase your watch time and your average view duration, which YouTube will use to promote your content. It's the little things like this that can make a whole lot of difference for you.

Key moments for audience retention are important to look at, as well. If you have a good eye, you'll begin to notice patterns in these types of analytics. If you have a series that is performing especially well in this category, consider taking a few minutes to watch these videos back with an unbiased perspective to see what about them is keeping an audience so interested at this point and try to replicate this across your other content. By doing so, you can once again increase watch time and average view durations. You can look through the Intro, which is the first 30 seconds of your video, or three other options: Top moments, Spikes, and Dips.

Top moments will detail videos where your audience is watching more for longer. These are oftentimes some of your best-performing videos. Spikes will show you the moments throughout a video where audience viewership spikes, often showing where viewers will skip ahead in videos. Dips will highlight the areas of your video where your audience retention is beginning to fall off, allowing you to realize mistakes that could be causing people to click off your video.

Top videos will also be important to look at. As these are your best-performing videos, it'll give you an idea of what works. By looking at these videos, you'll soon realize what topics or formats of content are working best for you. For me, gameplay commentary continues to work. It's up to you to determine if you want to begin replicating your best practices in these videos across the board in other content.

Top posts are important for channels utilizing the YouTube Community tab. You unlock this feature after gaining 500 subscribers. The Image tab allows you to see image posts you've made and how many times they were liked, which can be beneficial if you use pictures to cross-promote your brand. Polls are a great way to grow your channel: posting a poll per day can help you grow your channel by promoting your Community posts and polls to new audiences, who when they interact, will now be recommended your content in the future.

Text posts are also important. I personally use these to share updates on what's going on with my channel or brand. You can use these in many different ways, including to update people on new uploads who may not have notifications turned on or new audiences who can be recommended your Community post. Sharing your newest video in your Community tab can increase views and engagement at the same time.

Maximizing your engagement is what you're looking for here. What types of videos do you make that garner the most interaction? Do you have a series on your channel that makes people more likely to click the end screen? Are your Community tab posts getting any attention? Noticing subtle but important things like this can make or break your experience on this platform.

To maximize your engagement, you're going to want to do a few things:

- Encourage your viewers to like, subscribe, comment, etc. directly in the video. You can do this with a quick reminder or with lower third animations that you can get for cheap on Fiverr or from a digital artist.
- Use your content to make people have a reason to interact. Don't create boring, uninspiring content. Create something that inherently makes a viewer want to like the video. Making sure to upload HD videos with clear audio and relevant topics is crucial.
- As odd as it sounds - make sure to have engagement options turned on! Don't turn off comments, likes/dislikes, etc. Some creators do this because they're afraid of criticism or negative feedback, but this does nothing but create a fantasy world for you to live in and sets your channel back. Audiences want to interact, not be dictated how to watch content.

A popular way that creators have learned to maximize engagement is with what I call the 'Percentage method.' Here is an example:

"It turns out that only 40% of you are subscribed according to YouTube Analytics. If you enjoy the video and want to see more, make sure to hit the Subscribe button and turn on all notifications so that you don't miss an upload."

This might not seem important at first, however, this has become a proven and successful method of increasing subscribers and engagement. By providing statistics, the video can create a sense of trust with that creator and reminds the viewer that subscribing is an option. This method has been around for a while but is still extremely successful. You can also encourage people with similar methods to like or comment.

"Can we get this video to 10,000 likes? If so, I'll upload another video next week."

An Optimus video with a lower third card clearly visible. This one encourages you to follow my Twitter, though you can get them designed to do/say/promote nearly anything relevant.

Encouraging your audience to interact with your content is proven, and it's not 'selling out' or anything bad. Creators *need* their audiences to want to share and promote their content, so asking for them to do just that isn't pushing anything on anyone. All creators who are successful ask for engagement in some way, and while you're often told that this is what you'll need to do to succeed, there is somewhat of a science behind doing this.

You don't want to come off as too abrasive. My best advice is to be as 'relatable' as you possibly can when promoting engagement. Don't tell them that it's required or necessary, but try to naturally get your audience to interact by liking or sharing your content naturally. Many creators don't have to push this decision on their audience as hard because they create such high quality and entertaining content that viewers will decide to do this on their behalf anyway. Depending on what type of content you decide to produce, you may have to fine-tune this to find a perfect balance between being obnoxiously loud about engagement and being too quiet about engagement. Finding that perfect balance that doesn't annoy audiences away is going to be massive to the growth of your channel.

In the next chapter, we'll discuss the Audience tab of YouTube, breaking down the numbers behind the viewers of your channel. We'll discuss returning viewers, unique viewers, subscribers, videos growing your audience, competitors to your channel, and much more.

C19: YouTube Analytics: Audience

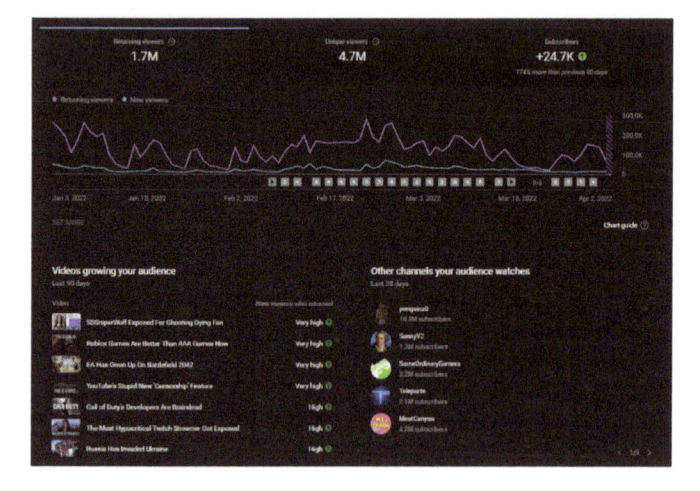

A screenshot of the YouTube Analytics Audience tab.

In this chapter, we'll discuss the Audience tab of YouTube Analytics to see what trends our viewers show us. It's important to know who you're being watched by. The more you know about your audience, the more you can do to cater to them and continue to grow your brand and channel.

First, let's go over some terms we'll see in this tab:

Returning viewers: The number of viewers who have watched you previously who watched your content again.

Unique viewers: The number of unique viewers/individual viewers on your channel.

Subscribers: The number of people who have subscribed to your channel.

Videos growing your audience: The videos that do the best at retaining new viewers.

Other channels your audience watches: The channels that you'll be competing the most with. Your viewers also really like these channels and will be watching them. Your goal is to keep viewers on your channel as much as possible.

When your viewers are on YouTube: An hourly schedule that shows you the hottest hours for your channel. Uploading during peak hours can lead to more initial views.

Other videos your audience watched: The other videos that were popular with your audience from other channels and competitors.

Top geographies: The top countries for your audience, which are marked by the percentage of total viewers.

Subscriber bell notifications: Statistics on how many subscribers have turned on all notifications for your channel and have enabled YouTube notifications.

Top subtitle/CC languages: The top languages and types of closed captioning preferred by your audience.

Watch time from subscribers: The amount of watch time generated by your subscribers compared to non-subscribers.

Age and gender: A comparison of the different age groups and genders that make up your audience.

Learning about your audience is going to be one of the most critical things that you can do as a YouTuber. You want to make sure you know just who you're targeting your videos to. Using these terms, you're about to be able to break the code on who watches your content.

Returning viewers is truthfully one of your most important metrics. This measures how many people are returning to your content to watch again, which will be crucial to developing a loyal and long-term fanbase that will allow you to turn this into a career. If you're consistently bringing people back to watch videos, you have a good shot at marketing other ventures and content styles to these same people. If you can't get people to watch your videos more than once, you're going to limit your exposure and views.

Unique viewers are also important. Having more unique viewers means that your reach is wider. If you can consistently bring in new, unique visitors, you now have a category of your audience to retarget. Bringing them back as often as possible is your #1 goal. Don't neglect to look at this metric as often as possible. If the number is increasing, this is generally a good thing. Not that having a low amount of unique viewers is bad, but the more, the better.

Subscribers are oftentimes what you first think about when it comes to YouTube. You want people to subscribe so that you can grow your channel, win YouTube Creator Awards, and build a number that you can be proud of. The more subscribers you have, the more leverage you have with your analytics. If you can get notifications out to 30,000 people consistently and 10% of people click it, that's 3,000 extra views on your video. When subscribers frequently interact with your content, that's when we get into our next topic.

Videos growing your audience might be one of my personal favorites, but is one of the most underrated features in YouTube Analytics. This teaches you what videos are most likely to turn new viewers into subscribers and consistent viewers of your channel. Looking at this allows you to recognize patterns in your content that you may have never noticed otherwise. For most channels, patterns will arise that allow you to easily understand what types of videos perform best on your channel.

If you have a popular series going on, then consider making more content similar to it or in that series. Be careful to not immediately convert your channel over to just this blueprint, however. You can be successful with multiple types of content. For instance, in recent months, videos talking about specific games and going over their current state of them have been very good for my channel. Also, videos where I talk about controversies or YouTube creator drama also seem to do very well. These aren't the same format of content, but both work for the Optimus YouTube channel.

Other channels your audience watches allow you to mark down your biggest competitors. These are channels that you'll be competing with for your viewers' time. Oftentimes, your audience is already watching these channels in significant numbers, allowing you to compare and contrast channels to see what you can improve. You may notice new specific topics or content formats that your audience could potentially enjoy, allowing you to immediately improve your content strategy.

Improving your content strategy will be critical no matter what stage of your YouTube journey you're in. Whether you're just starting out or have been doing it for 10+ years, there is always room for improvement. Noticing the best trends in your videos and in your competitors' videos is crucial. Use these to your advantage, because a good competitor is going to be doing so to your channel.

Paying attention to your top geographies lets you know what international markets you have to your advantage and lets you know what trends and content styles are popular in different nations around the world. You'll be able to see which nations contributed how much watch time to your channel and what the average view duration is there. For me, the United States is my #1 market. It makes up 59% of total views, has the highest average watch time, and contributes 62.7% of my watch time.

This is valuable information even outside of YouTube. When it comes to merchandise and other objectives, I know that the United States is where I should be focusing primarily. As a result, most of my merchandise sales and followers on other platforms are also American. I am American and speak fluent English, allowing me access to many other English-speaking nations, as well.

Subscriber bell notifications are a somewhat underlooked YouTube Analytics feature. It will tell you the number of subscribers that have notifications turned on for your channel. It will also tell you how many of these people have turned on general YouTube notifications, which are required to send push notifications. You can use this to get a good idea of what number of baseline views you can expect without any suggestions or recommendations. This should be the raw number of views you get on every upload period.

Top subtitle/CC languages allow you to see what languages viewers are preferring subtitles in. For me, this is English, and they're auto-generated. YouTube will automatically convert most videos to have basic closed captioning, even if you do not take action or upload your own. You do have the choice to close caption all of your videos, which is a good idea if possible. It allows deaf or hearing-impaired viewers to keep up with your content and is a nice addition to a lot of people's video-viewing experience. Personally, I always prefer subtitles as I like to read along and understand everything clearly.

Watch time from subscribers will give you a chance to see how much of the watch time is being contributed by your core audience. Ideally, you want much more watch time coming from new viewers in high amounts per person. This means not only are you marketing to a new audience but doing so effectively. Having a great amount of subscriber watch time is necessary to help grow your audience, so while you want more coming from new viewers, this is still important.

Age and gender can be useful metrics to help your content strategy and understand the monetization behind your channel. For instance, women and men are marketed to in many completely different ways. Depending on what you learn about your audience, you can begin to learn the shopping habits of your audience. This can be used to market merchandise and will be used by YouTube to serve more relevant ads to your audience.

We've gone over everything in YouTube Analytics that you'll use on a daily basis to develop a content strategy, build your audience and continue to propel your journey. Now, it's time to discuss a somewhat common question - what if it doesn't work?

C20: What If It Doesn't Work?

This is a common question: what if it doesn't work out?

Well, then what?

Sometimes, it's not going to work out. Remember the odds of you exploding on YouTube and becoming successful from it really are against you. You're not expected to reach even 1,000 subscribers. Even if you do everything right, you might just not have gotten the foothold in the algorithm necessary to blow your channel up. Alternatively, a million different things could've happened that didn't allow your journey to go the way that you thought it would at first thought.

This is okay! Not everyone is meant to do this, and it doesn't have to destroy your passion. If you don't make it to ten thousand subscribers, then so what? Continue to make content! Remember, it took me five full years to make even one dollar from YouTube. I didn't have a massive platform for over half a decade, that's how long it took me. It might take you three months or 10 years. You never really know when it could all come together.

So don't give up immediately. This is the trap that so many creators fall into and don't recover from. If you allow it to beat your psyche up and stress you out, then you've already lost. A major component of YouTube is simply to have fun while doing it. If you can't even do that, then you're already running into the type of issues that make it impossible for some creators to blow up.

Don't feel jealous about other creators having success, either. If you've collaborated with someone and they end up larger than you, then show them positivity. I personally believe in karma very heavily, and if you put negative energy out there due to jealousy surrounding another creator, then I believe karma will never allow you to succeed. Focus on yourself and your channel first and foremost and always make videos.

If you go around with the mentality of 'what if it doesn't work out for me' all the time, you're never going to progress anywhere. Part of doing YouTube is not giving up. Consistency is so important. If you give up now, you'll never see success later, and it's worth a shot. Even if the odds don't favor you, this doesn't mean you need to give up entirely and not want to pursue this.

This book is here to give up and coming creators some potentially new information and insight to help them increase their odds. I'm not here to guarantee your success. Even if I was, I could never do that. There's a pretty good chance it won't work out for you. This doesn't have to affect you personally or make you give up on trying. Also, don't be mad at me if the odds don't work out for you. I want to see you succeed, as well, and being mad that the book didn't 100% make you successful isn't helpful to either of us.

Sometimes things like this are out of your control. You can do a lot to try and fix it to where you have better odds, but that's about all you can do: try to raise your odds. You can't guarantee anything, especially on YouTube. Even if you do become successful, there's always a chance it can come crashing down. This is why it's important to continue to take care of your YouTube channel even after it becomes successful. If you don't take care of it, it can all come down tomorrow. Taking care of it means constantly learning about it, changing your strategy to how you see fit for growth, and constantly keeping yourself updated on changes going on with the YouTube platform.

If you're not willing to dedicate enough time to YouTube, of course, it won't work out. YouTube is a platform where you get out of it what you put into it, mostly. Sure, there are lots of creators who put everything into videos and never end up successful. This is a part of the process, and like I said earlier, unfortunately, not everyone can make it to the top or find continued success.

Don't blame others for it not working out for you. Continue working on your channel. Find new things to improve constantly. Create more content. Change up your process on how you create content. Try new things. Collaborate with new channels. There is honestly so much that you can do to improve your channel and its' odds of succeeding that finding people to blame for it not working out isn't even in your best interest.

For your sake, I hope things do work out. I hope you accomplish your dreams and make this YouTube thing whatever you want it to be. It's important to know that you don't have the best chances, and while it may be repetitive to say, it's one of the most important things to know. If you create a false sense of security in how everything is going to go with YouTube without even considering this is setting yourself up for failure.

With that being said, we're reaching the end of this book. While it won't be the end of your journey or mine, this is where we say goodbye to one another for now and wrap everything up. I've enjoyed being able to share all of this with you and hope you can find it useful. I'd love to see you do great after learning some new things like this!

C21: Farewell, and Good Luck

It's time for us to say goodbye to one another for now. I hope you were able to find some use in this book, and if not, I hope you enjoyed the history of my channel being explained in depth. Ultimately, I want this book to be something you don't regret purchasing. I want to be able to communicate ten years of my history with you all, documenting my journey that I'm proud of and giving you all the information I can on how I made it happen.

From here, you'll likely get to work on your YouTube channel, implementing new tactics that you might have learned from this book. I can't wait to see how they'll help you! They've all helped me tremendously in my time on YouTube. It's been a long time that I've spent trying to learn as much as possible and I'm so happy I've been able to consolidate it all down to the pages of this book for you and me.

My journey on YouTube has been fulfilling, challenging, difficult and incredible. Though I never expected to be in the position that I am, I'm very happy to be in it. I've accomplished my dreams. I've been able to accomplish another dream with this book, becoming a legitimate author and having my own book out. I've never taken this kind of step in my life, so it's definitely been a challenge. I hope that, at least for the first time, I was able to not disappoint you with this product.

I created Optimus on April 4th, 2012. In the ten years since then, my life has changed dramatically. I owe it all to you. Those of you who've watched my videos, supported my channel, purchased merchandise, followed me on different platforms, told your friends and family about my videos, and continued to support me in these ways even if I was inconsistent - thank you. From the bottom of my heart, this is the best way I could've ever imagined my life going.

To be here today talking about my ten-year anniversary on YouTube and to be able to share all of the information I've learned has been so eye-opening. I've been able to realize once again how much you all support me after you've bought this book. It's an incredible and surreal feeling to see the level of support you've all shown.

I wanted to take the time to highlight a few of the favorite comments I've received in anticipation of this book. These were sourced from my YouTube page:

"Congratulations bro, I'm sure you've worked your butt off for years to get to this point. Keep up the great work, I love your videos." - Jose Rodriguez

"Oh my god, I picked the perfect time to begin a creator journey. I'm about to start streaming and video creating. I know the basics but the more lucrative things such as sponsors or even just branding is so new to me. God this book would be a godsend, especially from someone like Optimus." - Kaleb Moody

Comments like these were instrumental in how I approached writing this. I wanted to give you all something of value that can help teach you something new. Even if you aren't a creator and are just interested in what goes into a YouTube channel, I wanted to provide you with the experience of what we have to think about on a daily basis. Thank you all for this opportunity, and God bless.

Going forward, I want to continue writing. I want to put out more books and provide you guys with stories that I've created. This passion for writing has been helped a lot by writing this book, which was a major step for me. I don't know if and when another full book like this will ever come, but I'll be back soon with something new for you all to enjoy.

With that being said, this is the end. I hope that you're successful and find what you're looking for in your journey on YouTube. I hope that my book was able to teach you something new, or at least entertained you for a little while. Thank you for your support on such a major venture...

And until the next video guys, this is Optimus... writing a book...

and signing out.